MW00620178

SO CLOSE

SO CLOSE

HÉLÈNE CIXOUS

TRANSLATED BY PEGGY KAMUF

polity

First published in French as *Si près* © Éditions Galilée, 2007

This English edition © Polity Press, 2009

Polity Press
65 Bridge Street
Cambridge CB2 1UR, UK.

Polity Press
350 Main Street
Malden, MA 02148, USA

All rights reserved. Except for the quotation of short passages for the purpose of criticism and review, no part of this publication may be reproduced, stored in a retrieval system, or transmitted, in any form or by any means, electronic, mechanical, photocopying, recording or otherwise, without the prior permission of the publisher.

ISBN-13: 978-0-7456-4435-6
ISBN-13: 978-0-7456-4436-3(pb)

A catalogue record for this book is available from the British Library.

Typeset in 10.75 on 14 pt Adobe Janson by
Servis Filmsetting Ltd, Stockport, Cheshire
Printed and bound by MPG Books Group, UK

Ouvrage publié avec le concours du Ministère français de la Culture –
Centre national du livre

Published with the assistance of the French Ministry of Culture – National
Centre for the Book

For further information on Polity, visit our website: www.politybooks.com

CONTENTS

"On August 14, 2005, I dealt my mother a blow, naturally it was unintentional, I would never do that myself, the most terrible part is that in the brief moment that preceded I had just been admiring her, she was in a bathing suit, I was sitting across from her, I admired the steadiness of her life instinct, I was not myself in a bathing suit, I hadn't thought of it, whereas my mother, as soon as she sensed the appalling heat rising through the windows, had responded to the danger, my mother never loses sight of a life whereas I am always losing them one after the other, the bathing suit had not moved, you see thought my mother, saw I, one must never throw anything away, I have had this bathing suit for thirty years, she no longer goes swimming ever since her skin is no longer her skin, we hadn't seen it in ten years, it is a one-piece, with wide diagonal strips, I was moved by the bathing suit, by the return of the bathing suit, by the reunion of the shimmering bathing suit with the henceforth two-toned body of my mother, whose pale skin is now painted with large ochre patches of various sizes and shapes 'it's beautiful' I was saying to myself, I noted the date of the unexpected apparition of my-mother-with-bathing-suit in my notebook, her wide, bare feet dressed with transparent bandages very flat on the floor, I was dazzled. The extent of the effect *mother-with-bathing-suit* has to do both with the event – the satisfaction for her of seeing her *throw-nothing-away* principle find a perfect application, for me of seeing myself see my mother again in a bathing suit something I had given up a few years ago forever, I mused while looking at her from head to foot, front and back – and also, I sense, with a vast zone that spreads out behind the event.

1

A zone I didn't have the time to explore, being entirely in the moment. Obviously I have feelings from ancient memories, I have silhouettes of long ago, but that doesn't interest me, I said to myself

my gaze was busy mentally photographing the desired face, the face of her birthday, I wanted to imprint in I know not what immortal wax my dearly beloved's features when she turned ninety-five years old, yet one more of those efforts that stretch all my energies raised to meet the death that is coming to our borders, I was given over entirely to this secret attempt to steal a picture taken from my mother in a bathing suit, I was hoping she was totally unaware of it, I was hoping to absorb her figure, this muscular drive of prey that makes its nest in me was brooding over this face in transformation, I was looking at the bathing suit then the face, *this* face is not her face, it is a face that escapes her, that apes her, she's not aware of it, there is a face that precedes her, propositions her, comes and goes nervously, seems always on the point of confessing, what, yet another one of those triumphantly incongruous thoughts perhaps, the wrinkles from bursts of laughter gather around those lips, like curtains on the two sides of the mouth from which truth will spout, I could spend hours contemplating these goings-on, and meanwhile in the middle of this feverish animation that lends her an unexpected charm, the two round, moist-brown eyes reflect faithfully, calmly, a kind of speech spoken by my mother's gaze, a profound and chaste summary of love. Deep within those eyes there is liquid starlight, a source that no mood swing or untimely whim ever alters. I was looking at the face then the bathing suit. And all the movements, this movementing of my mother is in a bathing suit made of elastic fibers.

Maman changes so quickly, I say to myself, this mobility is like that of a five-year-old child, I realize that this predatory passion keeps me captive myself, I want to take and I am taken by the need to take, it's a frenzy that devastates me, it's exhausting to want to hold onto what is passing, I am haunted by a mental camera, I who have never taken a photo in my life. Photography I've always thought is the enemy, my enemy exactly, the adversary, one can't take photos and write, I say to myself

Barely do I think this than my friend tells me exactly the opposite, there is writing in photographing he says, but I have never been able even to try, in the idea of taking a photograph technically everything frightens me, the idea of 'taking' whereas in my opinion the camera cuts, out of a photograph, the infinite flux of the untakable, whereas writing takes nothing at all, writing dreams of not stopping what is in the process of being lost, nothing more powerless and desperate, thus nothing more faithful to the infidelities of life I say to myself, we who write I was saying to myself, while trying not to lose the thread of the face of my mother who did not stop speaking for a second, which increased incalculably the speed of the changing expressions, we force ourselves through incredible acts of docility to receive, on the intimate surfaces that, like spiders' webs, are spread out by our hearts (for we have several hearts spread out in front of life, at least three ear-hearts, three tympanic organs, attentive to the echoes of Lives, when it is not simply the whole body that acts like a heart), the innumerable palpitations, hesitations, those twists of thought, those ripples of mood, that versatility of the interior climate which caused my mother to go from reproach to assent and vice versa in ten seconds, as if she were all the time several simultaneous goddesses.

From time to time I left the room, I went into the kitchen to make tea, during this interruption I gave my interior writing machine a rest, I waited for the kettle and I represented my mother quickly to myself just as I had seen her a moment ago, I recited her to myself, I could then be astonished by her rapid dwindling, every week she is losing physical density, but she is gaining in psychic flame, one has to imagine a candle that would melt not by descending the length of the wick but by slowly consuming its periphery. Then I went back to dip the pen that I am in the living room. I saw her once more, and I noted with sadness but joyfully this overwhelming thing: I open the door of the 'living' as we say, and my mother is there. In colors. Whereas the opposite will possibly occur, I was saying to myself. All of this, which weaves the warp of my life, and gives it a dramatic consistency, although apparently I do nothing but go up come down take a seat blaze trails through the forests of leaves, in reality I am living on the slopes of a volcano during the day, at night I travel through the caverns of the earth, I cover thousands of miles, it sometimes happens that I find myself in one of Plato's caves, without expecting or hoping for it, I am thus never outfitted as I should be I am wearing light clothing, whereas it is very cold in these halls where one should be protected, I shiver, I tremble and also I meet so many people from long ago that I haven't seen in an eternity, especially those with whom I had quarreled because they had quarreled with me, and all those old stories demonstrate on this occasion how ridiculous and overblown are our earthly plots. As for me, what interests me is the life beyond life, I should say the different lives that surround the one we call ordinary Life and that is life in common, measurable by the clock, declared on one's taxes, to the police, and in civilian life. I say these lives. They are certainly not separated from one another. They are adjoining, they touch, contaminate, propagate, continue one another

That I give myself over, methodically and passionately, to the study of the life of these lives of life, I can say it only to you, I say, to the Telephone. I speak a lot to the Telephone I thought, while quickly preparing a tray on which I set out macaroons for my mother. With that, I was no doubt

4

committing an error: she is going to refuse the macaroons, I said to myself, but that doesn't prevent me from trying. Otherwise, in advance, I would never offer her macaroons. Or bread. Or anything. So I set out the macaroons that perhaps, for once, she would not refuse.

Here is an odd thing: my love for the Telephone is equal in intensity and tenacity to my antipathy for the camera. That's because the Telephone is you. The camera is a prosthesis, it's a pair of optical pliers, an ocular harpoon, an avid prolongation of me

It sometimes happens that I telephone you mentally while I am sitting with my mother.

'No macaroons!' My mother – thrifty. What's the point of wasting a second by filling out a sentence? As for me I waste lots of time. She obeys strictly the laws of energy conservation. 'Macaroons? No!'

Meanwhile I too do two things at once: I phone you mentally. I describe for you the scene, called 'No macaroons!' 'Tell your mother that I too am against the idea of receiving macaroons,' you say. Later, in another scene I will discover the funereal secret of the word *macaroon*, and I will wonder, but in vain, if my mother knew about this, and how, through what strange telepathies or traces, when she brutally shoved away the little plate on which I thought I had placed some innocent cookies. I don't like macaroons myself but something in the word has always attracted me, without being able to decide if the taste of the word seemed good to me or not. At that moment we didn't know that macaroons are poison for the living. With caution I add: 'my mother is in a bathing suit.' I don't know if this is news. 'I'd like to see that!' says the Telephone.

All is lost, our youths, the delirious desire of the sea, the rebeginnings of the world, except for the bathing suit.

And then there are these dentures, I thought, these dentures drive me to the edge of the abyss, I can only say it to you I say to the Telephone, these days whenever I open my mother's door without knocking, all at once I see everything, I see the gaping mouth and the nothingness, I see the void that awaits me, for three surviving teeth she does not want to have dentures, this distresses me, not that I insist on dentures, not that I don't admire her will to die with all her teeth even if only three, but this eaten-away face that comes in place of hers distresses me I tell you, while preparing the tea I let go a sob – 'you must force her' you say to me, you too having or not having teeth makes you suffer, 'force her?' I say – 'force her,' you say, suddenly you are frenzied, 'you must make her' you say, 'you must convince her,' it is these teeth now that dictate our lives, my mother relies on them more than on her daughter, she believes her teeth, according to her three teeth the world is judged interrogated convicted just this once acquitted, preserved. – I bought fresh macaroons for her teeth I say to myself.

That's when I said *I would perhaps be going to Algiers*. There was no urgent reason to say this, that I know of. If there was one, it was hidden from me. I said, in a distracted, colorless voice: I will perhaps go to Algiers. I cannot even be sure that I said it myself. It's more like the other voice uttered these words as if to try them out. There was no tone of authority. Myself I heard the hesitation. The probability of going to Algiers was for me so weak. I did not say: I will go. The intention of going in any case was not there. If it existed, it was in the weakened form of a consent to external circumstances, which to be sure I had not yet given, I still had months in front of us before I had to do so. I don't know why I advanced this sentence toward my mother at that moment. Perhaps I was driven by the desire to hear myself say it aloud, as if I wanted to give the wandering shadow of this idea in my obscurity a little materiality, perhaps I said this sentence, to myself, by way of proxy. I believe that I didn't believe myself. It was only a sentence. I was trying out a hypothesis. But it may be that I wanted to test its resistance to reality. To bring it out of the shelter of fiction. I never had the idea of saying such a sentence. It may be moreover that it was the intention in me of not going to Algiers that drove me to cause the scandal to erupt. I was thinking only of myself, of my complications, of my muddles, of the mumbling of my will. I used my mother to do an experiment testing the validity of my hypotheses.

I did not at all expect what happened. There were cries. My mother had exploded. I can't recall how long it had been since I saw my mother rebel to the point of letting go loud cries that even as they seem to banish old age run the risk on the contrary of brutally accelerating the process of natural degradation.

It will now soon be thirty-five years that I have not thought at all of going to Algeria, I don't even think about it, I don't make any effort, I don't recall having first had the thought then pushing it away, when I think of the tension that filled my whole body while I lived in Algeria with the unbearable sensation of never finding myself inside but as if pinned to the outside of the inside, like a caterpillar forbidden to metamorphose, I thought then *in* Algeria *of* Algeria I heard its invisible music, I wanted so much to reach it, only a five-meter wall separated me from it, I spent my life looking for the entrance to the inside on the invisible outside wall on which I was clinging, an almostnothing of steel separated me from Algeria, this tension that was my whole being has totally disappeared, the memory I have of it floats all dried up without revivifying energy no more consistent in reality than the memory left by the powerful but ephemeral excitement I feel when, reading Balzac's *Adieu*, I cross without obstacle through the thin membrane of fiction, I inhabit for a few hours another soul, I go hunting, I find again the figure of the person I adored the most in the world and whom I lost at least so I have believed for thirty-five years, under the spell of the apparition, I swoon, I might then think when coming out of the swoon that *if* I saw Algeria appear in reality, especially if it had a curtain of black hair over its face, then it is I who would disappear, but barely do I return to my senses I really think nothing, I analyze nothing, I live finally from swoon to disappearance until the last minute of my story. I understand nothing and I will never have understood anything other than nothing until I die. There was a time. I know this time with a disused knowledge. I tried to arrive in Algeria, it would perhaps have been better for me if I had reached it, but it was impossible. So much so that I reached the impossibility, and this without having planned it. Today how can I not be gladdened by that? *To reach the impossibility* is neither a goal nor a possibility, it is an impossibility delivered in our absence. Did I ever think, hope, to achieve the summit of desire? When I was spending all my times climbing those walls, partitions, mountains, I did not hope, there was no future I was totally devoted to each instant, if I had hoped I would have been in despair. However, it may be that smoldering in me was the shadow of a feeling of vanity, one of those furtive forms of presentiment that one chases away with a puff of breath and to which one grants a status, belatedly, only when a catastrophe will have happened. To these retropresentiments of fatedness I have granted a decisive importance since 1993, the year in which I no longer succeeded in blocking the entrance of the Algeria-Thing into my books. To recognize that I had never thought I would manage to arrive one day in Algeria, in truth, and to attempt to manage to approach the Thing through the powerful means of literature, these two facts were produced during the same period. One can naturally recognize a long time later. I recognize in myself a kind of rage that surges up especially when faced with a monstrous misfortune whose event entails the destruction of the world. I am physically and mentally incapable of admitting this seizure of power by catastrophe this pure, absolute tyranny of what is unjust. I counter it with a dog's unbelief, a pagan's belief. I don't believe it, I call its reality into question. I did not believe my father's death, I believed more strongly in the opposite sense, I leapt backwards, I enclosed myself in another reality, one instituted by me. I maintained a very strong argument until the last minute. I would never have been defeated except by myself and that is what happened. I have always known that I knew he would not come back, but knowing counts for nothing next to willing, inventing, maintaining. What I know is nothing. It is what I will and am capable of (feeling) that is the true reality. I used to say: he is not dead. That was no less true than the contrary. Until the day. I have forgotten. The day I said: my father is dead, I don't remember. I close the book in which I lived, in which I died every day, in which I was haunted by the being whom I could never find again to the point of madness, and five minutes later it's as if nothing had happened. Adieu! Adieu, fiction which is the almighty goddess of our secondary states abandons us to our everyday mortality. These passions, these pains do not even go away. They return under the cardboard cover, become silent, are silenced, have never been. The passerby to whom one would recite the secret of this tomb feels no more pity than for a dead leaf. That is what death is: nothing remains, neither the memory of life, nor the memory of suffering, nor the memory of death, nor the memory of forgetting. Merely, in that vicinity, sometimes, a feeling of pallor, brief, flees. Nature closed its book again without a shudder. When one day opening by chance a volume of Balzac I read a short story called *Adieu* it will be the first time. The title, I admit, touches me because it is an echo of those bitterly tender and philosophical *saluts* addressed by Jacques Derrida to very dear friends. I will be able to cross through the translucid portal that separates me barely from these destinies. Without difficulty, with the naturalness I have in dreams, I will set out on the terribly steep and totally impassable path that leads to the summit of the mount, while tracing vertiginous loops, my own body will be my vehicle, my car, I will drive fast which will not prevent me from crawling at the same time, from testing often the soil of the trail and discovering with wonder its creamy and smooth consistency like a silky skin. Thus in the middle of the most desolate lands one can find an unbelievably soft thread. I will have the impression that I have already passed this way.

Since 1971 I have not reread the books to which I was linked in true friendship. An explanation? A thousand none. Too many explanations no explanations. I could recite them if I were asked.

All the things I do, without explanation, all the things I don't do, without explanation.

All the explanations one might discover will cover over the undiscoverable explanation.

For thirty-five years now I have not wanted to go to Algeria, I say to myself, I never thought of going there, I always thought of not going there, I wanted rather not-to-go-to-Algeria, each time that I could go to Algeria in the end it didn't happen, there are some countries to which I end up not going, I have no role in this, on the one hand I have my reasons, on the other there are circumstances, as regards Algeria it's not that I wanted never again to go there, I wanted rather to go there for sure, better not to go there than to go there in the wrong way, I couldn't go there in just any old way, it's much too dangerous, I have always been careful to hold onto to the hypothesis that admitted a trip to Algeria was probable, but I have always admitted simultaneously the opposite hypothesis: it could be that I will never get around to going to Algeria. In reality. In the first case I would hold onto what I call 'my algeriance,' a vast set of rather disparate reflections that arise around the notions of country, native country, country of origin, names of country and around this word 'country,' which burrows into the mind's wax and, into the heart of whoever says it, spreads *la paix et la pagaille*, peace and chaos, the one as much as the other. If one recognizes a country by the seeds it scatters, then Algeria is a great country I used to say to myself. I didn't want to go to Algiers and thus I would preserve intact the ideal beauty of the Jardin d'Essai, the Botanical Garden, in the form in which it was invented by my father in a first period then reinvented in another part by my friend Jacques Derrida, I hoped not to go to Algiers long enough, and thus be able to keep the Jardin d'Essai as a re-edition of Paradise on earth, and as unique and destined personal paradise in the form of a Garden of Literary Essays attempted by the one and the other. In Oran I had had the Inferno in the Garden of the Military Circle, then Paradise then death, in that order. I especially did not want to go to Oran, I'm afraid of losing the Inferno, one can also lose the Inferno, and how to go to Oran without losing my Inferno, my Hell which is situated like a worm in the heart of the adorable city. How, I gnawed at myself, not to go to Oran? So long as I don't go to Algiers, not going to Oran is natural. If I go to Algiers, how not to go to Oran, if I went to Algiers and I didn't go to Oran it would be brutal, it would be cruel, I would make myself suffer, it would be obscure, I would be unhappy, it would be morally inexplicable, it would be difficult, I can't just decide that I will expressly refrain from going to a city that I loved so tenderly, so what to do? All my life I have thanked my father for having moved us from Oran to Algiers after the war, for having deprived us of Oran, and thus for having given us nostalgia for Oran as an inheritance. In Oran we lived with my living father, Oran has always been the world before the end, the city that we did not lose, we left it in blazing glory. I especially did not want to go to Oran, which I had classified among the promised cities that I think about with an equally pounding heart, Oran like Prague, Oran like Osnabrück, but I would naturally do nothing to avoid it. My not-wanting is supple, flexible, it's not an interdiction, it's a submission. I do not give myself the order: you will not go. I let come what will come. I have an instinct

I have a fear of going to Algeria and of missing Algeria by going there of not finding it and thus of beginning having lost it, whereas I have not yet lost Algeria, I would say to myself, indeed I have never taken so much pleasure from the thing or the being Algeria as I have since I left there in 1971, beginning in 1971 I began to be able to think about so many ways of leaving and of coming, if I missed it that would naturally be my fault, I would have committed an excess of haste or delay or calculations and presentiments, it's better not to offend the soul with imagined things. Submission, that's the solution, one must give in I used to say to myself.

To go there as in a dream, that would be the ideal I used to say to myself. To go there as *a dream*, I dreamt. To go there in such a magical, intense, powerful, weightless, fugitive, total fashion that I would have been there even while being there as if I had not been there myself but another, with the force but the impunity, and even the immunity of a letter. If I could have sent myself, sent it to myself. Been it, the being, the letter [*L'être*]. It's like for the letter to Zohra Drif that I had had the idea and the need to write. I had thought to write a letter to Z.D. in 1960, perhaps it was in 1958. For the first time. I didn't finally write it. I didn't really think it either. I had as it were felt the light touch of a letter pass over me. It was clear but vague, that's it, it was the beginning of an impulse, one goes and then, no, but it would have been written clearly to Zohra, in the gathering of the circle it's I who lacked precision, I had the desire, the quivering wings, the letter fluttered at my window, not very far not so close, creature of the morning's dawn, then I rose and I thought I had perhaps dreamt it. I will write a letter, it will be impossible, dear Zohra I am writing to you, from which moral political ethical philosophical point of view I have no idea, I have always dreamt of blowing up trains and walls if you do it I am doubtlessly happy because the inadmissible thing is admissible the blood that you speak is the same in my language, next the ideal would be to blow up the separations I wanted to tell you but my voice was separated from me it would have been necessary to begin a sentence by we I don't have doubts about the impossible, what I have most despaired of you are doing, I am on the left side of your dream, you realize almost all the irreparable desires that it made me so sad to have for nothing, if I am not you are

next I will reread this letter, it will be crossed out everywhere, I will have to block out almost all the words, that is, the words will block out their meaning to me, I will split them, I will zap them with a Z, I will zoom over a hurdle, I'll take a breath, I'll not advance, what do I have in common with Zohra, except the silent weight of fits of anger in the classroom, I will open the door we can blow up the door, everything impossible will be easy, I will write: I am amazed I see the just person, which I will never be, I see her resemblance with you, I am not against blows from a golden lance and the exultations of bombs

while I was living *in the letter*, sometimes in my place, sometimes in the place of Zohra at least the one whom I imagined to be Zohra, a happiness took hold of me, which never had I or have I known elsewhere. It was a happiness of relief. What this happiness contained was triumphant. I can thus enjoy a happiness that is not mine, I can be in the freedom of someone else, I can be free because of another liberty that Z. takes for me.

The letter is a mess. No one can untangle what I think from what I think. Violence, justice, revolt, courage, right, everything gets all tangled up.

What is certain it that it stayed with me. A letter that I did not write. There are dozens of letters that I did not finally write to my beloved, that I was going to write, that I wrote passionately during the night, I signed with fire, I got up, the letter returned to the other world. They did not stay with me. I realize today that the letter to Z.D. is the only one to have reached the ineffaceable.

The idea occurs to me at this moment, August 15, 2006, that perhaps the decision to go to Algiers was made already with this letter and by all the innumerable, imperceptible circumstances, gestures, consequences contained in this sheet of paper, under the name of Z.D., perhaps this letter that has stayed with me has mingled itself with me, its totally invisible phantom atoms have spread into those regions about which we know nothing where our future events foment, so much so that the decision taking shape slowly, being secreted for decades, will naturally have the slow irresistible force of an accumulated seism that has been brewing for a thousand years. But this is only a hypothesis.

The fact remains that no one today could say whether I wrote *the letter to Z.D.* in the end or whether I did not write it in the end. I put *time* into it. That makes any evaluation difficult. With time the letter will not have failed to change, and often. In the beginning it was an impulse, but a tenacious, seductive one. I saw myself writing in five minutes an enthusiastic spontaneous letter. Rapid. Because of its improvised character, I would not weigh my words. The idea that it would be a total surprise for Zohra did not embarrass me, between us there were none of those virtual spaces in which letters might appear, moreover the idea that we knew each other only superficially had no weight, my impetus, my soul's passion swept aside these considerations. I could thereupon surmise that Zohra on her side could not have the least idea of what was stirring within me, since 1951 on the one hand and since forever likewise. It was objectively impossible that she had the least intimation of my Algerian turmoil. All these ideas that might have cut off my impetus were dispersed in the blink of an eye by the breath that animated me. What prevented me from writing this letter, which, to put it in a nutshell, was a burst of laughter, a jubilation rather than an argued missive, was the question of the address. I was nineteen years old perhaps I was no longer in Algeria, to say I was in Paris would be an exaggeration, I was in a state of mist, but in the corridors of Paris. Everything solid, brilliant, bleeding, sparkling, breathing, carnal was in Algiers, in Paris I floated in a gaseous state, I dragged through the dust, I didn't breathe. The sky? Terrible. So even the sky can be sullied by the soot of a country even the clouds suffered from a lack of lightness. To come back to Algiers, to Zohra, to the letter, I didn't have the address of Z. Not-having-the-address of the person to whom I wanted at all costs to write was how I always was in Algeria wanting at all costs to speak to, touch, find I knew exactly what and whom, but I didn't know how, *where*, to reach them, the telephones were always cut off, the iron gates raised in an exaggerated way up to the first floor without doorknob, without doorbells, the street names unknown, and it was starting over. If only I had been able to write to Z.D. in care of the Lycée Fromentin where we had been in the same class three years before the letter. But that was something one must not do. The letter would not be transmitted. I would not be advised. I would fall into the category of one of those destinerrancies whose tragic models I have seen to my sorrow, before finding them gathered malevolent identified as the very fate of humanity, under that appellation invented by my friend J.D., all those letters that are supposed to have arrived, and with which Shakespeare, Balzac, Stendhal make literature weep, those promises of life, which do not fail to get lost and which are transformed into messages of death, they are veritable bombs. The *lycée* was not my friend, it was Zohra's enemy, it was neither a post office, nor a home, our ex-French theater anti-Zohra on the one hand anti-me on the other. The hypothesis that I could write to the Prison, 'Z.D. Prison' – which one? – seemed to me a version of the letter addressed in care of the Lycée. It was probably good sense. I saw everywhere hostility, rejection, scorn that would greet on the one hand a request signed by the one who I then was from the point of view of the enemy, on the other hand the addressee considered otherwise but from the same point of view. Two different combined hostilities, one addressed to the neitherthis northat, judaic, exdeFrenchified, reFrenchified being which was my image seen from the French Fromentin point of view, the other turned against the Arab Muslim being, ex-boarding student at the Lycée Fromentin from there moved from one day to the next into the recesses of the Casbah from which she exits with her basketful of fatality – there was no chance. Logically. But I wanted my letter to arrive, or rather, I wanted it not to be stopped on the way. I could no longer address it except to 'Zohra Drif, Algeria.' I was thinking all the time of *good sense*. What is good sense? I had been thinking about it continually since the first philosophy lesson in the last year's philosophy class at the *lycée* when the teacher quoted the first sentence of *Discourse on Method*, so as to lead us comfortably, peacefully through the door of Reason, into a clear, happy reassuring, unshakeable French world. She had emphasized every reassuring syllable in a clear and reassuring voice, wanting to give us the good news right away: good sense is the most widely shared thing in the world. Although. I looked at her short, gnarled fingers, on those lips twisted by the desire to persuade there were beads of saliva. I was struck by a cosmic dread. I expected everything of philosophy, I had been waiting for years for philosophy as for salvation, the triumph of raw, bloody, naked, savage, fearless truth. With the first words I was overcome by anxiety. I saw the path of method, and that they were telling us to start out from good sense to go anywhere else, but that in order to go elsewhere one must start from there, from the most widely shared thing. But I was on the side of Proust, although without knowing it, without knowledge, by passion and enchantment. I turned around, I was always in the first row and right under the nose of the attacker, that is to say, the teacher. I tried to see a face. My anxiety ran around the class. The class was Catholic, as usual. In the back of the class, to the right at the back of the world, I thought I saw the face of Zohra Drif. It was surely an illusion, but a vital one. I wanted to see a face. A face is the least widely shared thing in the world. The one blinded of Sight who had been waiting for the philosophical light for years. I was waiting for a face. I couldn't see three yards in front of me, but that doesn't prevent seeing otherwise. In the urgency and dread that the first sentence of *Discourse on Method* had caused to explode in me, I speculated, intuitively. If today I had to sum up in a sign the being Z.D. in the space called Fromentin, it would be: a *frown*. There was always only one frown in the whole class: it was Zohra. Later I might say: a visor. That is, a Visage, the thing that goes into hiding and then suddenly appears. I wrote: *Non credo* on a scrap of paper. Folded in four. And I passed it to the other end of the world of the class. Or else I said to myself it's because 'good sense' is not good. Or else it's the most that is not the most, the thing that is not the thing, I was beside myself. I was waiting for a letter for years. And that was it, here, now, good sense in the Lycée Fromentin in Algiers, in Algeria, under France.

Had I not just read that the narrator of *La Recherche* quoted this 'good sense' that Descartes talks about as "the most widely spread thing in the world," the narrator, or else Proust, had replaced *shared* by *spread*, which changed absolutely everything, I would have given a lot to know if it was the narrator who had made a voluntary or involuntary error in *À l'ombre des jeunes filles en fleurs*, a book inherited from my father's library, where someone, a hero of French language and of thought passing through French, had not just *changed* the word but at the same time, while quoting, had dislodged the opinion of the one quoted, with an exhilarating modalizer's trick, saying, I quote: 'No doubt, it is not good sense that is "the most widely spread thing in the word" it is goodness.' I read that, while trembling with excitement, and these sentences that lent a hand to this trick of the hand, extravagant, magical sentences that in three dizzying lines exiled the whole indisputable dignity of philosophical authority, for everything changed, at least for me, depending on whether it was the fictional character or the author who was the author of this displacement replacement. So apparently there was France and the other, another than France? In Algeria, and more specifically at the Lycée Fromentin where I thought I was in a piece of France that was more representative of the France-Thing, more adherent to the spirit of France, than an embassy, *each utterance* having come from history, from culture, of the France-country where I had never been, where I had not been born anymore than anyone else in my families, and yet where flowed the language that I desired to adopt the most in the world, which I adored for its paradoxical riches, its deep sources of amphibology, its winks, its duplicities, seemed to me to hide a clue, an explanation, or a cause of the illness shared by the great majority of the inhabitants, a widespread and cunning illness in the minds, in the streets, the shops, the institutions, the interiors,

the most widely shared thing in the world that is to say the worst thing was hypocrisy, like second nature

No, I don't believe Z. answered my *Non credo* note. At least I don't remember it. This note moreover was not a letter.

If I had had the address of Z.D. in prison, what would have happened? I don't remember exactly what I would have written mentally. I do remember my state of mind: I was under an enchanted spell, I believe. Finally, I said to myself, this letter that I couldn't send anywhere has nevertheless gone out unbeknownst to me. No one escapes the principle of destin-errancy. I never thought about it again. Later I wrote 'Letter to Zohra Drif.' I can still see myself writing this text very quickly, I was happy enough with it, it came to me as if dictated, which happens to those who lead a life in the world to be written, I wanted to express something of the mysterious Detour that has always been inflicted on me, the originary malediction weighing on my relation to this native land that has never been my country except in literary utterances, and I heard being dictated to me this Letter to Z.D metaphor of my Algerian countertemporaneity. And right away this 'Letter' was published in French and immediately after in American. I thought I had found the means of translating the famous Detour into the two languages to which I confide my uncertain, divided human condition, and more precisely the languages where I lay down as in cradles or hospital beds my severed being. For I am severed from Algeria, ex-rooted from Algeria, and reattached for life to the French language. At that time the name of Zohra had distanced itself from Zohra. When I titled this text 'Letter to Zohra Drif,' the name of Z. had a range that had gone beyond Z. to come closer to a certain Algeria for which I was not nostalgic, that I loved because it was not mine, because it was she because it was not me, because she was another, because finally time had separated us, I was not in Algeria it was not in me, she was not in prison, I could think of it, of her, I didn't even know how to write her name. I didn't know where to put the *h*.

What seems to me the most important, I say to myself, is the returning-Detour effect of this text. There is a turn in the genre that resists analysis. The letter is a letter that is not sup-posed to be that [*l'être*], nor bound to be a letter and to which it may happen to be received as a letter. Is it an open letter? If Z. reads it, which cannot be completely excluded – if Zohra exists in reality, Zohra is still alive – which I was able to verify – once Z. read the 'Letter to Zohra Drif,' this singular literary exercise would instantly become an open letter to Zohra Drif I said to myself.

All the same, if I declare: 'in fact it is not to Z.D. that I had written this letter' I didn't write it to the person of that name whom I had known in the past and never seen again. The genre of this 'Letter' was of a unique kind. That, from the viewpoint of literary convention, it was an open letter because published, I do not deny. But what does 'open' mean? What interests me is the expression: one says 'open' and not 'public.' Just because it's 'open' does not mean it is not 'closed.' I had written a 'letter' to someone who would never read it, I thought. There are letters whose destinerrant trajectory one believes can be calculated. On the basis of the projection of this route one establishes a text with risks, a part of which remains knowingly incalculable. I had thus written this letter addressed to one of the characters of the person Z.D. without the intention of reaching the person, at least not in my lifetime, I say to myself. And this certainty, which was unstable but sincere, gave me pleasure of an exquisite kind, of the sort encountered only at the undecided frontier that is drawn and erased between the different regimes of reality and probability. Did I ever expect a response? Which response? Whereas conversely the 'Letter to Zohra Drif' was a response. Not that she, Z., had written me a letter. As I see it, when we were at the Lycée Fromentin in the same class at opposed angles me in front to the left she in back to the right, *she was a letter*, and I was *the other*, I had to be it [*j'avais à l'être*], I felt it, I wanted to respond, I was desperately seeking how to respond. I had been condemned from birth, by my genealogy and by the catastrophic worldwide circumstances

20

whose result and heir I was, on the one hand to be *always the first to speak* in front of the so-called French French people from France and the so-called French French people of Algeria, that is, 99% of the French present, the upshot being that I never hesitated. If there were French hence believers, I charged. In the Fromentin classroom as soon as a lesson began *I spoke first*. As soon as the teacher raised her voice, I had to speak. If the professor was doing Juno, I did Echo, the one in the first chapter who spoke faster than speech. I had to block the French authority. To the question how can one be born [*naître*] in Algeria without being there [*en être*] since the dawn, how can one be neither [*n'être*] from Algeria nor from France while being all the while in a counterfeit, a simulacrum of a country, in pseudonymity, in simulacrity, alone? to this question, I was condemned to respond with a strategy of velocity. I had to get free of France in the person of the teacher from France with a sentence that left her uncertain

On the other hand I was condemned inversely *never to speak first* in front of those among whom I was born without being born from them, the said Arabs later called Algerians, I would have been cross with myself if I had taken over the speech that was not mine but that should have been theirs first and to which access was constantly held behind bars, thus condemned always to speak first on the one hand and in the same place to listen to the speech that might come from the back of the class to the right and for which I was destined to be an Echo, one who left her body to keep only her voice, Echo the second. For example when everything about Zohra cried out: 'Ecquis adest?,' I saw clearly that her way of asking *if there was not someone here* was the expression of bitter doubt, ironic, no, it would not have been possible for her to say *is there someone* she expected that the response would be no one and as for me all I could do was Echo, enraged shadow but too slight that I was, saying: *et adest*. It wasn't much, those

21

cries. Is there not someone *here*?, said Voice Z. – *Here*. That is what Voice H. responds. Here. I cooed. Echooed.

Voice Z.: Whose cry? – Voice H.: I. At the Lycée Fromentin we are good in Latin. A dead enough language. It's to be read. A repose is kept in secret by the dead. A peace forever young, a stunning beauty for having been plucked alive out of the wars. I am avid for Ovid, like everyone. *Carmen perpetuum*. The song is perpetual. We pass on. Suddenly we are exiled. The song continues. From afar we write open letters to the Far. 'Huc coeamus.' Come let us reunite says the Letter. *Coeamus*. Unite us, I wanted to say.

In the end one writes: Nite us. It is so late, so far. Us. I fulfilled my mythological duty, I say to myself, with so much delay, remains only the echo of echo, but so faint, but as early as possible. I had to dig a tunnel beneath destinies in order to pass along a little of the music of the errancies. As early as possible and very late, I replied, plied, I said, sad, this time is not mine, no time is mine, there remain here only a few shadows, my mother, and the books that know no age. 'Whoever you are who touches this neither private nor public letter, deprived of address, may it at least be granted a place in your life. Tell yourself that it has not been included in the complete works of its author, but that it was as if torn from the tomb . . .' I had thought of adding these lines of postscript *sed quasi de funere rapta sui*. I changed my mind because of 'the tomb.' 'As if torn from the tomb' calls for an explanation. One doesn't know whose tomb it is, one never knows whose tomb it is, I thought, one never knows whose Letter it is, I never knew, it has always seemed to me that I was born 'as if torn from the tomb,' I didn't want to have written a Letter that ended with 'tomb'"

. . .

22

had I written.

What is Zohra going to say?

I am already extremely worried, I am not light-hearted, I am going to be seventy years old one can't say that I say that to myself with the amazement of Stendhal discovering from the top of the Janiculum hill in Rome all of ancient and modern Rome, Rome in Rome, Rome after Rome before Rome, and while counting on his fingers, fifty years, a thousand years and fifty years, discovering that he was going on his fiftieth year, at a joyful pace, having just thought about Hannibal and the Romans, at fifty one is seventy, to which one must add a thousand years of Rome and Carthage, the tomb doesn't keep count, it is ageless, he is of every age, me I say to myself just the opposite, I can't say that I am on the points of exclamation, I am neither straddling nor prancing, I am sad, "greater ones than I are dead" I say, but the tone's not right, it's not Stendhal's, Stendhal who was so reconciled to the mortal condition by the mere fact of seeing himself alive resuscitate Rome on impulse, in 1833, from there, seeing himself resuscitated in turn in 1924 by someone, as for me I have trouble resuscitating, at least resuscitating myself with Algiers, I already strain to go back to the top of Santa Cruz and thereupon I shower reproach upon myself

I must already struggle page by page to tear myself from the tomb, and thereupon *what is Zohra going to say?* I had already written everything that precedes, going forward with

23

these dreaded steps backward, by successive rewinds, I am helpless against regrets. I stopped here: page 37.

I leafed through the volume. The pages were numbered from 1 to 10. Then between 1 and 10 I saw that I had placed pages identified as 1A to 1G. This series had been followed by some 1AIs that had stuck themselves into different cracks of the volume, I saw that I was now on the next series of pages identified by 1AI *bis* to page 1JI *bis*. Between page 1 and page 10 had been inserted nearly the length of a book, I saw.

I was in that anxious and fatalistic mood in which dozens of times I had seen my friend J.D. plunged when on reaching a page 150, he woke up at the bottom of the page to the reality that had stayed well hidden until then: while he was moving toward the heart of the beginning, he had just discovered that time would soon be up, worse the organizers of the conference had granted him two hours to speak, which were long since passed, is that really possible?! at that moment he was reaching the fifth hour, this unforeseen discovery caught him up short "for after all," he said, "have I steered my life in the smallest way whatsoever?" exactly as Stendhal said in 1833. Naturally, I say to myself I can't manage to write this book. I noted on July 27, 2006. What is my daughter going to say?

– You never manage to write your books. – My torment is new, that's what worries me. I'm not in the process of writing the Book-that-I-do-not-write and that I will never write, I thought, I'm afraid of being repulsed from this volume by a secret force that comes from the Subject. I recognize the sign: every time I tried to write "on" Algeria, there was a disappearance-compulsion in my first pages of notes. I state the facts. They are small, but awful events and endowed with extraordinary obsessional powers. (1) I cover several pages with notes. Their scope is so profound that, seeing already the whole book, in germination, satisfied, I take a rest. (2) On Tuesday the pages can't be found. (3) In a third installment I spend several days looking for the pages that I know from experience can't be found. (4) Instead of using these ultra-precious days writing. (5) I drive myself crazy and the thought crosses my mind that I am in the process of committing suicide. (6) My daughter gently asks me on the telephone: did you find them again? (7) No, I say. I don't think about it any more.

Naturally, which is to say literaturally. I can't manage to drive this book along, I say to myself. At that moment I saw myself arriving at the sacred mountain. J.D. offered to take me to visit it, he says to me that he has been there himself. It's true that he knows Algeria much better than I. He led me to the summit that looks out over the three parallel ridges whose grey slate rock has the brilliance of steel. It's not very high. It's sharp. This is where everything began he says to me, the sacrifices, religion. It's beautiful, I say. I thought so. It's for tourists, he says to me. Come. He was going to show me where it was *really beautiful*, and that in general no one saw. We went a little further through the woods. Here it is he says. In the rock you could see a fast-running stream, fish of stone were going down the water current one after the other. It's here that everything began. It's here that it is beautiful, says my friend. I thought everything was beautiful despite everything including the schistous mountains as sharp as blades, and that I was far from my beginning. "What is Zohra going to say?" This sentence prevents me from writing what I'm writing. I couldn't pretend that this interrogative sentence and this thought had not suddenly struck me. She thinks that I am writing a book on our Algeria, on our Algerias, a wonderful subject, a unique story, the book of two lives, a book in two books, which is what I should do, I am not doing it at all. I have always been pursued in my books by sentences that get me in trouble, beginning with *What is X going to say?* This is the first time in forty-four years that the subject of the sentence is not someone in my family. Now not only am I responsible: before and for my brother, my mother,

25

each of my children, my beloved, my father, my friend J.D. who has never failed to ask me: "what does your mother say?" and especially: "what does your brother say?" but here now the idea of Z. has made its entrance. I should have expected it. There is no pure outside, there is no pure inside.

I am perhaps in deepest Algeria when I think I am still climbing toward the summit from which I believe I'll have a view of the whole of my book. *I should leave it at that*, I say to myself.

I try to avoid the metatext. Everything is metatext. I try to exit: I enter. I enter: I exit. When I was five years old, at the Oran Opera, I used to dance blindly on the stage among the throng of dancers and singers I was inside, at the end of the ballet I could no longer get out, I could never find the exit. There was one. Already it was impossible to find I wandered around the basements, I crossed though rooms both large and small, I thought about the city of Oran that was outside and to which I had lost the entrance which was also the exit from the Opera. I exit.

The idea of wanting to see Algeria one last time, that's one I will not have in any case. It's an idea of death. It would mean that Algeria is going to die. If it was I of the two who was going to die, I would naturally keep my death to myself

I start over.

In a certain way I thought of going there *naturally*. I thought I would go there before the end. One time. The end would be that of a story. I didn't have the intention. I had the thought. Finally I would end up by going there. I lived on the hypothesis that I would indeed end up by going there. I didn't think that I would return there. There is no return. It would be something else. A kind of visit, I would go and *I would let myself visit, be visited*.

Yet it is possible that this may not happen, I said to myself, Jacques Derrida, my life friend, will finally not have gone to

Algiers, in those last years, since forty years earlier we had said "Algeria," hundreds of times, we came and went constantly around the theme, we thought sometimes of going there sometimes not sometimes perhaps sometimes never we walked our shadows in the streets of Algiers each one his or her own streets, we walked each other in one Algiers or another the same one but not at all the same one, no one has ever seen two such dissimilar cities I have never seen his Algiers I said to myself, Algiers was not at all like that he said to me *your* Algiers he used to say, I used to say *your* Algiers, we found ourselves in the same lecture hall, at the same table, just one microphone two different cities, I have never seen *Youralgiers* he used to say I used to say, you see all one has to do is change the street, the neighborhood, and the only point at which we met was the Lycée Bugeaud, the same *lycée*, where we had been one after the other one before the other and that was the same. We had been one after the other in the same class of Advanced Literature and years later I thought exactly the same things that he had thought in the same class, but at that time he had been in Paris for a long time while I was still in Algiers, I was sitting at the desk where had had sat but I didn't know it yet and the day we discovered that, so late and by chance, we didn't have time to go into the classroom that was all the way at the top on the next floor, after the monumental staircase, along the hallway to the right. This staircase had the enormous proportions of a staircase built to make one feel, as one went up and down its immense steps, that here a totally other world began. One could not have taken that staircase without mutating. In 1949, in 1954. Going up this gigantic staircase, one saw oneself arriving in Paris, we used to say. You raised your head and you were surprised by the height of the vaulted ceiling, by its classic arch. Each year a class entered to take the place of the preceding class, one went to Bugeaud to enter Paris at the top in its upper schools, the names of the predecessors were repeated in the class, by waves a mythology was constituted, the frequenting of ghosts was always part of Bugeaud's staircase, but I didn't hear J.D.'s name repeated I entered too late to inherit from his predecession. A year at Bugeaud. We used to say: Atbugeaud, we didn't know what we were saying. I am *atbugeaud*, and there was something about it that made one hear nothing. Atbugeaud for a year during which one was already no longer in Algiers, one had stopped thinking Algiers, one did history, there was plenty to broaden and enlarge one, the history of the church in the nineteenth century, the invention of the cult of the Virgin Mary, that happened atbugeaud, we traversed the nineteenth century, we thought we would soon be in Paris already in Paris that is to say Athens, that is to say the future that was already there beneath the porticos, Socrates is on the boulevards next year we'll be modern and Jerusalem philosophical, and that was the Error. Class after class, arriving in Paris as a consequence of Atbugeaud, from one day to the next it was the small deportation, the instant degradation of the dream state, we were absolutely not made for the Paris-Thing. In less than a week we had discovered with terror that we were made exactly against, that is to say made to be thrown against Paris, and that Paris was formed for the demolition of the presumptuous ones coming from Algiers, we left Bugeaud to go to the Demolishing and we didn't know it, mowed down row after row, some in a famous *demolycée*, the others in a minor *demolycée*, these were apocalypses. Suddenly one was from Algiers, we had never been so obviously so profoundly beings from Algiers. You opened the door you went into one of the rooms of the Paris-Thing, and you saw. At first glance you saw yourself. Too late we learned that we were children of Algiers, at that moment we were invaded by a feeling of immigration, but once started toward Paris, there was absolutely no possible turning back, one couldn't go back down the

28

staircase at Bugeaud. The gigantic and dark staircase of the Lycée Bugeaud had indeed been the antechamber of the New World, the hold of the ship *France*. Once entered Atbugeaud impossible to return to Algiers. Impossible to find oneself in good shape in Paris. Not to go to Paris was impossible. AllAlgiers knew the terrible story of Pariente, the philosophical genius who had believed and AllAlgiers believed with him that he could reach the summit of Paris by making the climb in Algiers without passing by way of Paris, such a genius, the greatest in Algeria, had preceded J.D. AllAlgiers spoke of Pariente the Titan, who could take the exams in Algiers and who had been eliminated, swept aside both him and the illusions of Algiers on his first try. AllAlgiers had learned with astonishment that the greatest philosophical champion of Algiers was nothing when seen from Paris. AllAlgiers had failed with Pariente once and for all. After the fall of Pariente no one ever again thought it possible to achieve entrance to Paris from Algiers. AllAlgiers said: don't do a Pariente. One had to present oneself for the exams in Paris. All the titanic forces of AllAlgiers were nothing for Paris. All the immense bare-footed and shirt-sleeved forces. One had to present oneself in Paris and abjure Algiers. The decapitation of Pariente was the first fall of Algiers. One had to leave Algiers. Paris has always autodecapitated itself of Algiers. If one wanted to have a head one had to go up to Paris to seek it. AllAlgiers lived decapitated. I have never known Algeria with a head. I used to think. I have always lived in a headless country

"I could have put on the black one" says my mother. "There's not really much choice." That's when I said that I might perhaps go to Algiers, and my mother shot off: "Without me!" as if it was I who had shot at her. Vehemence, that's her, Ève. Evidently she claims that it's me. – "You, when you say Osnabrück, do I yell?" I yelled.

29

Osnabrück says my mother. She says Osnabrück and there's no harm done. She says all the time "Osnabrück, we". She often says: "at home in Osnabrück." Never will I say: "at home in Algiers." "At home in Oran." Then one day I wrote a book called *Osnabrück*. Naturally *Osnabrück* began to call me to Osnabrück. I think about it. I try to imagine a book called *Oran* or *Algiers*, I can't do it at all.

When I said to my mother: next year we will go to Osnabrück in June, she said to me: by train. Not by plane. Why not by plane? One goes to Osnabrück by night train. I set aside the fact that we argued about the hotel. That's part of the journey.

I set aside the fact that all the same we didn't go there. I returned the tickets. That's part of the journey. But when I vaguely said *Algiers, perhaps*, she yelled: "What-is-this?" That warlike way she has of sticking all the syllables together in a single guttural apostrophe. "Algiers" I say. "I said Al-giers," I said. "What do you think I said?" "I know what you said!" "What?" "And what does that mean?" "You think I don't know what it means?" "Algeria?" says my mother." "Never-any-Algeria." One has to imagine the music. Astonished voice, rising, come from the depths of time, attaining the high pitch of incredulity. Pause. Voice goes back down the slope. The Algeria question, abyssal, suspended. Algeria? she says. What is "Algeria"? The thing is but a word. A strange signifier. "Algeria," I say, louder, "And in dreams? Do you dream of Algeria?" I insist. "Never-any-Algeria" says my mother's voice. What could that be, the Algeria-Thing? Algeria never says my mother. Algeria leaves. I retain two sentences without verbs. The first opens, the question calls: Algeria?!! The second closes. It's the beginning and the end. Hardly begun finished. Algeria, how's that? Finished. Even in dreams. My mother shuts the door, so as to make sure that Algeria has no chance to sneak into the room, the window also. I laughed.

Whereas I continued to live on the hypothesis that in the end I would have gone once to Algeria.

Withoutme! My mother's war cry. She laughs. Tries. Her hair in disorder, she knocks her spoon on the table. I will get the upper hand, I'm sure of it, what am I without my mother, and without my mother Algeria, I see my mother running at me, her ninety-five years surround her and guard her prodigiously.

I didn't see myself, I felt a terror break out on my forehead, on my eyelids, as for her, I saw her protesting to the heavens which I had just soiled according to her, trembling with furious sobs against all those who have constantly betrayed her, the family's dead who never lent her a hand, and now me, the greatest catastrophe had struck for her birthday, it's as if I had crossed out her whole history, I took her umbrella on which she leans as she does on my arm and I broke it into a thousand pieces, she says, I never asked anything of anyone, she says, in vain you ask me to go to Algiers, she says, you will go *without me*. And in front of my eyes that didn't know where to look, so as not to see the violent nakedness of the damage, she became the being Without Me, a gnarled, storm-whipped incarnation of a person thrown in the mud by her loved ones. "Algeria?" Today you are upright, I am down in the mud. Tomorrow you will in turn be without me and in the mud. In the midst of a whirlwind of limping, half-blind regrets, I glimpsed as if projected onto the door of the room a metallic door of an elevator or a prison, I don't know, a frightening image. On the door there was an immense photo of my mother, obscene. I have little, ruined eyes, I am strange, nothing helps, her head appears enlarged, a meter wide, as if better to frighten me, it's thrown back, the mouth open on a scream and the three teeth, which are also enlarged, are planted there like fangs, but wobbly. She is at once hideous and adorable. I am staggered by the violence of this theatrical staging. A single

31

sentence and one calls up the most monstrous visual acts! And there I am facing my mother's gaping mouth! Something must be done!

Something! Say something to me! I must be on my knees before her because I see the back of her throat. Then my mother says in a voice sharpened by an infinite resentment: "*I've not f'gotten.*" She doesn't say: I have not forgotten. That would already be to forgive halfway. She stamps out the words I'venotf'gotten. She throws the verb *Ivenotfgotten* in my face. We're a long way from the peaceful beginning. Then she looks for a way to strike me even harder. She finds it: There's not afffucking thing for me there. She slams down *FFFucking*, with the small satisfaction of feeling the word fuck around between her lips, that's new, she has never spurted out that word in her whole life. I may take pleasure from this event, later, when I recount it to my friend, but how far I am at this moment from the blessed time of any story. There is no literature in the room. I didn't know where we were going, nor how long we were going to suffer from being in transit, I will tell him, I thought trying to hoist myself out of the situation, but I couldn't escape from the blaze while leaving my mother to consume her Without Me without me.

I was ready to pay any price at all, to pray any prayer at all, in order to appease my mother's fire. For all the rest I no longer knew what I would have wanted to desire or imagine. I made a sacrifice, therefore. – "I want to go see Papa's tomb," I said. The lamb's throat is cut. I had just sacrificed my secret, the most fragile and precious secret, the virgin secret, the one that I myself do not come near, the one that I do not tell myself, the one that I succeed in ignoring, keeping it dormant in the most obscure part of myself, the one I don't think about except in dreams, the very wish itself the wish that I can never wish for, a frail and tiny ghost of desire more like a small trembling of the heart than a formulation of thought. I had just broken vows so sacred, so secret that I had never even pronounced them. Never since my real life began had I tried, never had I gone, never had I tried to see, never had I thought to try to go to see my father's tomb. I trembled as if I had just allowed my arms to be torn off, to let be torn from my arms the adored body that all the same I had never embraced. I had confessed the treasure that I had never touched. And why had I given up the Tomb? I had tried to divert my mother's sorrow. I was ready to swear to her that I would not go to Algiers. The word Algiers had been called up only by metonymy, I was ready to swear it. I had not wanted to say that perhaps I would go to see my father, or else my father's tomb, that is, my father by metonymy, or else the metonymy of my father, the most unbelievable, mysterious substitutions get produced within us, one thinks one is going to such and such a city but it is the most subtle way of not going to such and such a city, I saw my mother's tensed face, on the day of her birthday, I absolutely could not try to explain to her what I myself felt I didn't understand, I will leave that to my friend, I reproached myself sharply for having uttered such a sentence, which was so unnecessary, at least apparently, and on that day between us, and I repeated with a little more conviction: "I want to go see Papa's tomb."

And right away the passionate desire to "see the tomb," which I had never felt, overwhelmed me, rose up beneath me, to the point that I could almost believe I had never thought of anything else. And yet, the idea of discovering this desire in front of my mother on the day of the bathing suit is something I cannot explain. No doubt I could find a dozen explanations, unpleasant ones for the most part, but I'm convinced if there is a decisive, indisputable one, it remains well hidden from me. I said: "*I want to go see Papa's tomb.*" I portrayed the role of daughter in the classic tradition for which I felt no sympathy, but all the same there was perhaps a little bit of me. And my mother said: "*The cemetery does not need you.*" I admired her. I admire it. This infinite sentence, from the moment it came from my infinite mother, whom I admire, this sentence assaults me with the finite so long as it remains near my mother's lips, this sentence sharpened on my mother's tongue, by means of which, with one good blow, it tries to put an end to my mental suppurations, it aims to discharge my heart. I put myself in her place and I hear this woman who has not gotten over weeping for Papa as she nears her seventieth year, that is to say, my seventieth year and this in the face of her own ninety-fifth year. My mother. The other (one). Fortunately no one sees us I say to myself, this scene has no witnesses, it is one of those strictly private scenes, which grants it a certain frankness: it is free to be obscene, grotesque, pitiful, violently anguished anguishing and this without any obscenity, without willing, without calculation, for we do not know what we are doing and what we are saying, we are stripping each other and mutually, we are in the skin of nudes who have an astounding strength for their age, we are thrown into a fight between wild beasts, my muzzle was full of earth and bones and my mother's tail was sweeping the ground in a threatening sway. Then the beasts locked their enormous horns, they began to push each other back with their heads, to paw the ground, in such a situation it is in principle the stronger one who wins, often the older one, but not always. But in this case each time one of them began to back away, at the point at which the other was going to be able to assert her victory and her authority, at that very moment of the one's defeat, the other softened and began to back off,

she can't see why she would go to Algiers, she can't see why she would not go to Algiers, she can't see why she can't see why, she can't see why she can't see

34

wherever I turn always in front of me is the thought
of death

death is nothing I'm afraid that death may be nothing

I look every which way and I think I see it coming, I see
nothing and that's it, it's coming, it's coming, that's all it
does, comes, comes between, makes come, nothing more

greater ones than I are dead
greater ones than I are indeed dead
I'm afraid of not having the strength
my dead are greater than I
where will I find the strength
to annihilate their death

"While my mother lives" I say to myself

"The cemetery does not need you" she says. The sentence
opens up before me like an equivocal invitation. Should I
enter? Who needs whom? I was delighted with my mother.
Her idiomatic genius – she doesn't realize it. All of a sudden
the Cemetery became a powerful and formidable character in
this scene. We were in a courtroom and my plea was rejected.

– You imagine that you have some importance for the
Cemetery? my mother made me think.

Thus my mother made herself the Cemetery's interpreter.
She speaks for it. It gets along without you, she says to me,
it's not the Cemetery who needs you. If the Cemetery is a
subject, one may imagine all the ruses of the utterance, I say.
But I don't dare say what I think: my mother is jealous of the
Cemetery. She lends it the feelings she wants it to have. Her
obscure wish is that the Cemetery will reject me, an apt pun-
ishment for one who mistakes the Cemetery for her father,
instead of making a trip to the supermarket with her mother.
But perhaps she merely wanted to say to me: it's too early to
die. One doesn't need that.

– So go ahead, says my mother.

– You think I ought not to go?

– Where? says my mother. Go ahead, says my mother. What are we talking about?

Now the horns are so interlocked that if you try to get free you only entangle yourself further. At that moment my mother ate a macaroon. That saddened me. Right away I ate a macaroon.

– Too sweet. Says my mother. So it was only a macaroon.

Beneath the quite living teeth of my mother the macaroon has lost its funerary power. It became nothing more than a four-penny pastry.

I was relieved.

– I don't see what possible interest it could have, she says. Me neither, I say, I don't see the interest, there is no interest, it's about something else, which is not visible and has no name.

I saw that I had thought perhaps of going to Algiers without knowing or seeing or calculating but moved by a reflex contraction of the soul, I had even said "Algiers" without attributing any precise and excluding value to the word, I had said: Algiers, the way one says threshold or Prague or yesterday, or the part for the whole. I was not even born in Algiers, I say to myself. In Algiers I died for the first time. As my father, through his death, I am from Algiers. I was thus born once in Algiers by survisection. I remember having said "Algiers" by way of attenuation, I didn't want to say "Algeria," so as to avoid marking some interest for a whole country, I had been content to say: Algiers, and I didn't say Oran. Yet I was born in Oran. But I have always declared that I will never go to Oran. If there is an eternal city that I never want to touch, it is Oran. I can think of going to Algiers, I can think of not going to Algiers. Algiers is outside me. I can enter then leave, I can go enter leave, I see myself standing at the edge

36

of the postcard of Algiers above to the left the immense bay
is below, I see myself leaning on the balustrade that borders
the crest of the immense bay, I see myself looking at Algiers.
Oran is my urn. I am inside. In its vapor. I could enter there
only if I had gotten out of it thus if I got out of it. I cannot get
out of Oran: Oran is in me; naturally and reciprocally, *intus
et in cute*. I cannot look at Oran from above. I cannot say that
Oran is me. I am Oran's. How then could I go there?

When I said "Algiers," I didn't mean to say precisely
Algiers, I don't know exactly what I wanted, the point was I
think *to approach, as much as possible and as little as possible,* by
way of metonymies, by intuitions, by detours, to approach,
but what? Not the City of Algiers. Besides I would have
to know what a City is. Not the country of that city. Not
the name Algiers either. A long time ago I gave myself the
names, to write, hundreds of times I have gathered, combined, sown the letters of the names in my texts, these names
Oran, Algiers, Algeria whose letters are very fertile when
mixed with French. No need to go there to impregnate my
language with their saps and their salts while adding in those
of Osnabrück, the OranAlgiers of my mother. I can say that
I have subjected all these proper names to fascinating emul-
sion and ebullition experiments. I have made them foam.
Foams are objects that are almost not elementary at all.
While mixing the letters of the names of cities I have found
myself everywhere at once, very quickly, I have witnessed
unprecedented transplantations, nothing is lost, nothing is
created, everything is transformed. And yet some conservation keeps things from destruction. There is conservation. I
have observed phenomena of extraordinary textual dilation
and excitation, language and all the thoughts it embodies
have grown in height, in volume, let's put twenty centimeters
of milk in a tube and let's heat it, the thing mutates emulsifies
and rises to five meters, perhaps ten, then words flow over the

edges of words, into thought, into imagination, is it still milk, ex-milk, what is foam, what to think of foam, what to think of the foam of thought, thought foams I say to myself, as soon as it subjected to the feverish heat that reigns in the frontier regions, where life enters into transformation on contact with its limit, nothing is lost all is transformed

I had hit the year 2005 and I had been hit by two thousand and five years and more of humanity busy thinking and not thinking – body and soul and languages under the yoke, relaying one another and sweeping one another aside from generation to generation – upon approach to the partitions of time, some of them, philosophers for the most part, spending the whole duration of their lives thinking about each letter, word, spacing of the duration, of the hard and the soft of duration, of the finish and definition of life, of living and not-living in pitched struggle in life, of the division of life into lives of variable duration, of the separation of lives in life by the blades of death, of the repairing of the irreparable, until their last breath and then ... others waking up all at once to thinking about thinking starting from a certain moment, suddenly, as if they had just gone through a door leading to the time of Emergency. And I am of this latter sort. All of a sudden it is Late. It's raining Time. There is no longer any stopping the rain of Time. There are Times everywhere and each time different, Times of all kinds and all colors

This time I didn't say "Algiers" because of the city or the name, the point was to *approach*. It was to *get myself closer*. Myself to myself. Perhaps out of the desire to get closer to what is kept secret from me. A Place-Thing that calls me but mutely, that I feel calling to me through pulsings of my blood, an emergency. The Emergency. Nothing gets lost, I said to myself, but if I was reassured by this promise, I was no less terrified by it. Nothing gets *itself* lost, things don't lose *themselves*, beings don't lose *themselves*, it's I, I thought, who

38

doesn't save them. I let distances grow. My desk, my head are overrun by distances and distractions. There are abysses nearby. I suspect the Nearby of being conducive to holes.

Worse: I have let _the Python_ in. I remember how startled I was when for the first time I glimpsed it, slithering almost invisible beneath a page of _Albertine disparue_, I first noticed slight ripplings in the paper, it just barely wrinkled. There was some "it" dozing there, there was something too calm about this calm. Around me the cats set off the alarm of their fattened tails. The narration slowed down, it held my breath. Daringly but carefully I decided to go alone down those sentence paths. Although the page isn't large, it is formless, it crawls by circling back on itself, there is a danger of getting lost and not being able to leave ever again. I had gotten to "that great intermittent force, which was going to do battle in me" when I heard a meow of distress. I look around. I see nothing. Meanwhile the call was insistent. Help. I follow the words by ear, I was thinking all the time of my mother, of Albertine, in my anxiety I could no longer find her name, I wanted to call her, I managed only to tear an Al-! out of the silence. I was going along and then, after "could no longer suffer for . . ." it's there. What do I see? I approach. I lean down. It looks like a dog buried alive up to the snout. I see a yellow muzzle. And a long body as if covered in sand. Full of pity and at the same time anxiety I lean over. And I felt a panicking horror within me. The beast is not buried. It's a double dog a little lionlike, in the eyes, a siamese beast suffering atrociously wounded, dying without dying, who looks at me with despair, with one head in front followed by another head on the spine, a long body follows from there, I don't know if it inflicted its own wounds, one head biting the other back. A feeling of desperate powerlessness and pity overwhelms me the beast sees that I feel its pain but I have no idea what I could do to comfort us. I am a stranger in this book and yet. Should I finish it off?

The wounded, degenerate double lion starts to tremble in the page where it's been enclosed, "he noticed all of a sudden the python that will devour him," I read these words and I am totally disarmed, I have just recognized the only enemy who can defeat me, but this python is me, this obliviated thing, this doubled thing is me, I am suffering horribly from devouring, myself, my own heart. That day I had to leave it there. I noted the address of the Forgetting. It was page 31 of the first chapter. Right after that I lost it. I had to go off in search of this scene several times. I was insatiable. I must have found something again, but I don't know what. Was it the panic, the pity, the python? I wanted to understand. I ran into the forgetting. Each time after exploring the narrative at length, if I saw a page take on an excessive calm, I returned to the place, I read. I tried to observe the cruel work of memory, I never again found the entrance to the cage quickly enough to cut short my anxiety.

Now the Python is at home with me. It is black and rolled up in the closet in the form of a monstrous macaroon. I don't see it.

I look at my mother while suffering what is only the fore-taste of the suffering that awaits me in the kitchen when I will go in there later, and when looking at the cabinet I will not see on its door the bright pink post-it on which she wrote last night: "coffee in the glass jar in the fridge," I'll see nothing, I'll not see that there is no post-it. I might even Forget my mother, I say to the Telephone. Saying it to you is the only way of saying it to myself and I insist on saying it to myself: it's the only way to try to resist Forgetting for as long as possible, the only way to delay it, to see it come before not seeing it any longer for once it succeeds in invading the closet, in curling up its monstrous and formless body into a limp macaroon in all the closets it will be from then on one with me like the Python with the Proustian narrator, and I will spend the rest of my days digesting what is dearest to me in the world. If at least we knew how to think Forgetting, but it's impossible. Let us observe Forgetting, I say to myself. And right away instead of analyzing it, plumbing it, anatomizing it, I respect it, I transfix myself and I am forgettified.

One can even forget one's mother in full daylight, I say to myself. Knowing that and fearing it I work at annoying my mother, setting her against me. When I said: "I will perhaps go to Algiers" in the bedroom, I warned my mother. On the one hand, I ought to have left her alone. I could have left from one day to the next. I would have betrayed her for the sake of her peace and mine. But I have always preferred that she be warned. I have always given her the chance to defend herself and accuse me. When I said: "I will perhaps go to Algiers" I had ventured into one of those hypersensitive regions, one of those mythical forests where trials and revelations await us, encounters with wild animals, with mad knights, abandoned fiancées, royal stags that seem the incarnation of dreaded parents, heads of State, and from which we don't know with what conviction of innocence or crime of condemnation or redemption we'll exit. I said the sentence while preparing myself to cancel it, withdraw it, doubtfully. What stopped me is a meowing of distress and it was my mother.

I have never dreamt of going to Algiers. Me, I prowl around Oran and it's paradise. My mother avoids, in vain. She returns to her Clinic, to do what, it has no relation with reality, then she wakes up and loses her Clinic once again. The elevator still doesn't work, she says, even in a dream. Since she was expelled, the elevator has stopped. Each time I return to Algiers, I see people who no longer exist, she says, it's to be avoided. This dream says my mother is like the lawyer whom one must avoid. You have a lawyer he tells you sleep soundly, I'm taking good care of your affairs. It's OK as long as your eyes are closed. You wake up you have nothing left.

As for the lawyer, he's changed his address. Algiers, says my mother, is what ends badly. It forced me to leave quickly on the sly, with the littlesuitcase, instead of defending myself and by defending myself defending the pregnant women and thus the future of Algeria. Lost causes are lost. No dreams! says my mother. No lawyers! I said at the time the earthenware pot against the cast-iron pot is not worth the trouble. I dream of Algiers it's a cast-iron pot that is an earthenware pot, says my mother. As for me, I prowl around Oran there is no pot, the narrow streets flow like golden syrup toward the sea, the lions sleep on their paws in front of City Hall, the reality of the noble square always has the same steamy substance, I have always floated over Oran, everything that happens in Oran has always been instantly awakened in dream.

I've not f'gotten, says my mother. You forget, go ahead. Me, I've not f'gotten that they stole my clinic. 1971 didn't leave me with good memories. There's not afffucking thing for me there.

I think about this. To steal, to be robbed, a complicated subject. Someone cut off one of my mother's heads.

– But you did go back to Osnabrück, I say. In reality, in dream and in one of my books, after having said to me "I will perhaps go to Osnabrück" at which I don't recall having meowed, whether you went or not, as there is not much more difference between the idea of going to O. and the idea of going to A., than between the idea of going to O. or A. in reality and the idea of going there in dream and likewise no big difference between the memory of a city in dream and the memory of a city in reality, the essential thing for me consisted in the modalization of the *perhaps*, I liked that you might have gone there perhaps. I say. And likewise I would like *perhapstogo* to Algiers, to see. – It's not the same thing returning to Osnabrück where I lived my whole life, said my mother, and I said nothing because my mother lived less time in O. than I did in A. but the truth may be where one doesn't see it. If my mother lived her whole life in Osnabrück, I thought, surprised and saddened, her life will have then been very short. Or else after leaving Osnabrück forever at the age of nineteen she will have stayed there in dream her whole life, which I have just discovered. – Me personally I have nothing to do there. If you believe you owe them something. – *Them?* I say. – *Them*, says my mother. – *Who them* I say? Maman, can you tell me whom you are not naming? I say. – *Them*, says my mother. If you believe you owe.

Because of *them*

Because of the anthem heat we don't go outside.

Because of that and because of the bathing suit and because of the buzzing of a wasp, and because of the memory of a former coolness in the darkest rooms.

I thought of the blue that makes up the sky of Algiers, then of the orange of the sky and the gold of the sky in the sea in the Algiers dawn

and because of these sensations

of Zohra.

What-is-Zohra-going-to-say is now one of the sentences of this book. It traverses it at regular intervals, floats, stops, moves on, among the upper branches of the pines, a little dimly luminous stellar formation, I see it to one side in the background behind me. I recognize it by its withheld breath, since it murmurs I can't hear the color of its intonation, it wavers, perhaps perhaps, I recognize it it's the figure that my surge of guilt has chosen for this book, or else it's the book that has chosen it for an emblem, thinking that this might help me in my guilt. To add to the confusion, I might then ask myself in the book what Zohra would say about this meta-textual incrustation *"What-is-Zohra-going-to-say"*, either in the book or in reality. From my side the inscription shows me the force of Zohra's impact on my unconscious when Zohra and I met. That I am marked by it does not naturally entail that Z. is equally marked by H. Of course the name of Zohra designates more than one animated being, Z. is Algeria thus the unknown about which I have been thinking since I left it/her since she/it left me always in advance and which upsets everything I try to think. I bear down on the point Z. so to see myself from the other point of view. It is not easy.

Owe struck me. I had not thought of that. Right away I began to make a list of what I owe to Algeria, mentally first of all, later I carried over into one of my notebooks what rushed to form several twisted and broken columns of a ruined forum. I summoned myself to answer as philosophically or else as honestly as possible, because of the word *owe* that my mother threw at me. Someone says the words *owe* to me, and thereupon, ineluctably, I feel I owe a response, one of those little courtrooms with well-worn woodwork always ready for my persecution opens up, and even if I am in the middle of the forest I begin my speech for the defense.

OK, then, I must try to make my way along the steep red heights whose interior rock always has the slaughtered ox color of the primitive cliffs, those great Oranais jaws along which I thought I would lose my small child's life.

My mother says to me: *owe* and I am owed. My state is that of Henri Brulard at the Saint-Bernard pass. Except for the high spirits, I arrive at the pass or the cut as if I had to choose between two ways of succumbing.

On my left, the reasons to go to Algeria. On my right the reasons not to go. All of them, covered in fog, and beneath these indistinct layers of shifting pebbles, irregular polygons with sharp angles.

I advanced without knowing. As philosophy advises. At each step one sinks in, words pivot, beginning with the word

Algeria, then the word *them* that referred to an indefinite community. It's because: "I was born in Algeria." I hesitated. This is a fact. Should I file it on the right? Or on the left? Naturally, to each his or her own, there are millions of Algerias. That I was born in Algeria is a fact which is, from a certain point of view, indisputable. I will never deny having been born-in-Algeria. All the same I just have to say these words: "I was born in Algeria" to feel a slight ungluing of my being, like a sensation of contraband, and even a hint of novels, something that resembles a genre, as if this sentence were a quotation, the beginning of an autobiography. Just as Osnabrück, no matter how disappeared forever it may be, seems to me to belong solidly to the Jonas family, just as the signature Jonas of Osnabrück seems natural to me, so with everything connected to the being Algeria, I am timid. I had just written "I was born in Algeria" and once again I felt that I didn't know what I was saying, what this sentence was saying to me, I don't know what it was thinking by saying "in Algeria" or borninAlgeria or what I thought of being born in without being of, being of nothingness, not being of Algeria, but with Algeria nonetheless. I felt this uncanny and exhilarating strangeness that has the gift of repeating itself, reigniting itself with each interrogation. I was astonished. Each time I make my declaration I astonish myself. Yet it is merely a fact and probable. And yet within me a slight incredulity arises. It is my status as specter that crosses my skull and with its light touch unglues all the modalities of believing.

 Zohra as well was born in Algeria I say to myself. There is no doubt. And that is the difference between Z. and me. Between my being born and me there is doubt

Millions of complicated thoughts, an enormous quantity of memories for many screens, powerful and solemn legendary scenes that happened in a background between the venerable and eloquent monuments that raised their sphinx-like busts

what is the allegory for Algeria?
long history?

read allegory p. rosma

don't think

around the Place d'Armes, great deployments of war, I recognize that for thirty-five years an _Allegory_ has taken the place of Algeria in my head. And before the allegory was produced, I have no other memory except so profoundly planted in the folds of my flesh, so engraved in my personal grotto that, as soon as I say this sentence, I seem to be in the antiquity of a fiction I invent and whose invention I am. I forget myself. I would not swear as to my authenticity. For example I see all these people who live in France and are sure of being Algerians, and I don't see myself as one of their number. As soon as I say "Algiers" there is a danger. If I say France, it's less troubled, I am outside. Algiers is always taking place in the subsoil, and I have always had to enter there because I have never been there, I have never _found_ myself there, I have always had to _enter_ there by crawling, either by going through the cracks in the shape of half-open mouths in the famous flesh-red rock as if I were a letter, or else by shrinking myself so as to slip between the bars.

I suffered thousands of times and even every day when I went to the _lycées_, first to the Lycée Lamoricière where the war's little Jews had just been reinjected after having been ejected from the land, ex-nationalized, excreted, legally execrated, then reinjected still all sticky into the Military School with its walls padded in Catholicism, then to the Lycée Stéphane Gsell where I never arrived without having first gotten lost in the mountains of motionless fog among which the Golden lance of Joan of Arc kept watch, then to the Lycée Fromentin where from war's larva I passed without knowing it into the subterranean corridors that were going to lead me to literature, it could not have been otherwise, I went from the veiled abyss to glassed-in margins, a book in hand, where I soon noticed, in a corner of the classroom in the back to the right the absolutely exact face of the one whom I, on my side, would never be and in whom I recognized in a second under the name of

Zohra Drif the inversely symmetrical being from me. And it was beginning from point Z. that I could begin at the Lycée Fromentin to crystallize in a less delirious fashion and in the open air my being on the other side. After having been buried during my very long childhoods in the underground corridors beneath the Algeria of France, for I can say retrospectively that I was born beneath this Algeria of France, I always knew as soon as I attained the first elements of knowledge that I was born destined to the hole and the cellar, a presentiment that I was forbidden from confessing for my first three years by the innocent jubilation of my parents on earth. Nevertheless this light that I saw did not last long enough, barely a year, for me to believe it was a natural phenomenon. I realize quite well that my parents were able to believe they were in Algeria, especially my father who was really born there and who since 1908 had not ceased to progress in this belief of being-of and -in, raising himself by degrees, in one of those ascending and harmonious academic arcs that makes one believe one is going toward the Universal Rose and that it exists. Especially Eve my mother who having gotten herself out of the German hell was able to believe she was part of it upon finding herself young and strong again in Oran. Whereas I from the beginning I saw that they were dust and I saw them return to dust, trodden beneath the soles of this supercountry where my father thought he had a place set aside. Whereas I always knew that for roof I had the vault of a cellar or a stairway. They rode bicycles on the land, they laughed I heard them, I contemplated their radiance, they were going to be extinguished and they didn't know it, I already had three hundred years' distance necessarily, the sun is going to set I thought with an anguish of worldwide proportion, and it happened. At the Lycées of the first General Marshall Lamoricière up to the fourth General Marshall Bugeaud I always went without illusion and without parents into battle against the Romans, in the beginning I was on Hannibal's side, later I discovered that all wars ended in dust, the greatest armies the greatest empires with millions of sorrows slept in a few paragraphs in the History books, of the hundreds of millions of men and women who were born, there remains a number with zeros in the mouth of a pupil among the chewing gum and the caramel he himself is one of the zeros destined to be chewed up again after a little turn around the track, between the teeth of the next pupil. Already in the *lycées* the butcher's block is readied and the very name of the Lycée called Bugeaud, if one paid attention to it, would have reminded the brief inhabitant of the fate of humanity. You think you are in an educational establishment, nursemaid of children. In truth it is a monument to the massacre. The pupils are sitting on the bones. I will not let them cut my throat without having written my will I thought.

– If I say to you *Né* [born], I say to the Telephone, what is it?

– It seems to me we've already talked a lot about this, you say.

It can be all sorts of things, obviously. *Né* or *Née*, masculine or feminine? Or *Nez*, nose? Or *Nais*, first- or second-person present singular of the verb *naître*, to be born. Since it's a monosyllable. The littlest words are the most pregnant with possibilities.

– Is it a phoneme? I say. – A *faune aime?* you say . . . A *faux nez*, a false nose I say. A nose is always a false nose.

– How do you write it? – *N-é* I say.

– How do you write "Né", I say to my mother. *Née* Klein says my mother. – The other one, I say. When you say "Né" on the telephone. "Ne! Ne!" –I say *"Né"*? – On the telephone when you talk to your sister. – I never realized it. –How is it written? – It is not written at all. It is also not said. – But when you say it all the same. – One says it but you can't write it. Perhaps it's said in our district of Osnabrück. But as for me I say *Nein*. No, I don't say *Né*.

48

I recognize that this word Né has haunted me for dozens of years. That's the way it is with phantom lexemes. It's like the Dé of J.D. It we knew where they want to lead us, would we follow them? The *dé* was written by AllAlgiers as DEY.

– I will perhaps go see J.D.'s house, I say to myself, on the Rue d'Aurelle de Paladines, another general's punch in the nose of Algiers.

I will go first of all to the Jardin d'Essai I say to my mother.

What I owe to them: my inexhaustible algeriance, my milk my formula: the wrath, the salt, the bitter, the laugh. My algirritation. All natives of Algeria are explosive. There is sulfur in the air. The odor of blood powder in the French class at the Lycée Fromentin.

(Zohra Note. *In the place where I begin the list, I put here the telephone call coming indirectly from Zohra, having its provenance in Zohra but suspended and diverted. It does not really belong on the list, but you will see later how it weighed on my decision as much and perhaps more than my internal struggles. In a first moment the telephone call took place, but I do not receive it. And yet it is not lost. At the end of the battle around the table with my mother I want to ask her for a ceasefire, F. comes by my house and gives me a message she received for me on behalf of a lady whose sister is named Zohra Drif. The lady says that her sister asked her to find Hélène Cixous at all costs and most urgently. In my absence F. decided to give my telephone number to this lady. F. asks me if Zohra Drif, who is the sister of the lady, has called me. No, I say. F. is astonished. The lady had said several times that she* must at all costs *find Hélène Cixous and* most urgently. Both things. Two pages later F. comes back. I place it here so as not to interrupt the state of siege in which we enclosed ourselves. No Zohra Drif did not call I say, F. is astonished. I tell her that urgency is an elastic concept, traversed with sideways motions, backward surges. In literature one meets up with thousands of examples of urgencies of different varieties. People remain in urgency for years, all of a sudden there are two*

*pages remaining, the author hurriedly causes a storm to explode, or
a bomb, something that falls quickly it's over. I don't expect Zohra
to call I say. F. does not understand Zohra, she does not understand
me. "It's Algiers" I say. F. does not understand and I understand
her.)*

Now we sit down at the rectangular table, my mother
along its length, me at its angle, along its width. I look at her
bare forearms the spots as large as my hand, wine-colored,
blotches caused by the clash between her illness and the
remedies against her illness that attack the patient, thus my
mother and consequently me as well who am in the middle of
this brawl. Then I look at the imitation Claude Monet oilskin
tablecloth that pleases my mother, imitation iris imitation
crocus I adore the oilskin tablecloth says my mother whereas
I detest the idea but I will adore this tablecloth and already I
adore it a little from adoring it later everything that I detest I
will adore after my mother, whose elbows blotched with large
spots the color of cortisone are leaning on two egg-yolk cro-
cuses. What a journey we are on, I will tell this to my beloved,
I travel non-stop round-trip present future future past imper-
fect past anterior present. A yellow crocus à la Bonnard and
I take off, the clock is mad the big hand turns in the opposite
direction from the little hand I advance backwards, I get my
tickets I cancel, it takes me thirty-five years to leave to arrive
in Algiers to manage-to-leave/arrive, surely it will have been
the longest journey ever undertaken in my life I will tell my
beloved who, as for him, naturally spends half his time in air-
planes half of which in airports that are microhells on earth.
Whereas for me the dining room is my mental airport. I am
seated with my mother. I get up, I consult the screen, our
planes are delayed until death I say to myself. It's the state of
the forearms, I say to myself, that urges me to go to Algiers, a
desire hiding a fear, the one smoldering beneath the other to
the point that you make many sudden movements, jumps to

the side or back, as if you had just seen the enemy. And then right after you leap forward. How much my mother is *against* it, I say to myself. My mother raised her teacup and I saw four big spots the color of dried blood on the inside of her left arm. At that moment I thought it was necessary that I go to Algeria as soon as possible. – Why now? said my mother. And I didn't answer, that was precisely the question I was trying to rule out.

As the end approaches our lives behave strangely like a book that, when it approaches the beginning, stumbles and tramples the space before the text in a manic and solemn delay, as if to put oneself into words was to put an end. This is what I, powerless but tenacious, have observed ever since I began to shelter in the house the idea of the book that would go to Algiers. Here's a being who is tormented by the idea of going, delay at dawn, delay at dusk, it cannot last any longer and it lasts it's a robust phantom, it goes up and down from morning till night, it mockeries my nights for although during the day it does not take off, all dreams pass by way of Algeria, it sits on a step before the door to my office, it spends hours playing with a word, I say delay, that is, *atermoiement*, I say it as I hear it, what have I done! yet another pretext to unravel time. There is a fate. It's not as if I could make this first or this last trip on the stairs. That would be a tragedy. It has happened. I know a poet who died on the stairs, so perhaps from the stairs, on the day he was leaving for a country from which he never again returned. All those countries from which one doesn't return to which one doesn't return to which one is going to return to which one returns so much in thought that it is difficult to know the difference between going, not going, and going not to go, one spends years in the lunar light of the airport. One is attached to it by the most ancient and dimly known pact, the pact of being one of the born or the dead of that country. There is no explanation. There is an umbilical

51

cord. It is a shadow of a cord, an immaterial cord the effect of which one feels planted in the cerebellum. We are the consequences. There are cells, says my beloved. As for me, I have been dreaming of going to Algiers for a dozen years. As a precaution I use the verb "going." My cells don't follow along. They act as if I said: "returning." I wait.

One shouldn't wonder why one decides from one minute to the next to cross from one side to the other because the reasons do not precede. The reasons are secreted during the journey. Why not before this day, why this day. It's always death that decides, I thought, but one doesn't know where it is, I didn't say that. Practically I had to depart leaving my mother behind me while she was still there, still leavable, still stronger than me, while she still persisted in countering me, in making me feel her disagreement, in ambushing my steps, in whying each of my gestures, it's because she didn't want me to go to Algiers that I was attempting my chance, as if I were siphoning the desire from her life and while my going away would distress her and would distress me as well, I was leaving only by walking backwards and with regret but all the same, as I've done moreover my whole life because my mother has never agreed with my decisions, I have always been in the opposite direction from my mother and vice versa, I have never been to the hairdresser's without having the feeling that I was cutting my hair from her head, but if I had given in on the hair, I would have given in on everything, I would never have made any cut, I would have long hair, I would not have written, I have thus always been in the opposite direction of my mother's whying, and it is this discord that has been the spring of my existence. Until the age of thirty I used to get violently angry with each disapproval, my misery was extreme I thought about breaking things off, then from one day to the next – following a scene where we flew into a rage at each other while swearing beating the cane of an umbrella against the low wall of a beach in Algiers (Moretti), and where I declared that I was leaving and would never again return, I would leave her forever alone in Algiers I didn't leave – the idea came to me, standing before the sea which, while we were shouting, intoned its calm rumbling, that perhaps all the misery I thought I found in the congenital confrontation was a happiness disguised so as better to preserve itself, that this pain was my inheritance, and the admirable manifestation of the natural forces of my mother. I look at myself in my mother and I see myself reversed. I sit down on the wall at Moretti, I look at us battling. I always have a little notebook in which I sketch us. Since the beach in Algiers I have always done what she advised me not to do, not that I follow her advice backwards, but I advance along the dizzying ledges escorted by her faithfully negative commentaries, it reassures me. Before every trip I pass through the bristly maternal arena so as to run up against her opinion, it's a brutal but brief traversal that I call "doing Moretti." That battle took place already thirty-eight years ago and since then I have my source in my mother. It's all very well to know the inevitability of Reproaches, it remains unforeseeable. In truth my mother explodes only when I don't expect it. Why now? I saw myself arriving before long at the foot of the maternal century, Time will rise to the heavens, there will be no crack and everything will become forever impassable. The feeling that slowed me down, still held me back, was the sad color of this urgency, I must leave without delay despite my mother thus with her powerful and weak presence casting wide dark glances at my back, I must leave behind me the little, diminishing body, in which the soul seems still more flamboyant.

for if she were no longer there, if I could no longer disobey her, if I could no longer leave without her consent, thus accompanied by her non-consent, a snatched benediction, fortified by her resistance that I would force myself unwillingly to overcome, if I could no longer leave with the very living image of my mother protesting her disapproval in Paris the city to which Algiers had exiled her, sitting down to write me a letter beginning thus: "My dear daughter, you are going to leave for what is called *eine Traumreise*" while I would be flying toward Algiers the city to which she had given thousands of births and which had from one day to the next thrown her to the ghosts, and thus with this flight I would be objectively on "their" side, forming by metonymy one body with Algiers, I would be a party to my mother's expulsion at least for a few days, I who had fled Algiers, she who had been faithful to it and for nothing.

– But what do you think of cemeteries? I said and I drank a mouthful of tea.

– You and your cemeteries, said my mother. Too strong!

My mother pushes away her cup of tea, she doesn't move it, she rejects, I say to myself. Waltz of the cups. I am outraged, silent. I wipe up several drops splashed on the oilcloth. And in the end she said: Too late. Ninety-five years old. *Out!* says my mother's hand. She has more and more authority. Get out! Take it away! Stop! She expels. The way she was expelled. *Fort! Raus!*

– One shouldn't put them in a coffin.

I was extremely sensitive to the savage beauty of this sentence. I would gladly have noted it down. It's like when Rimbaud begins by "These are cities" and before "These" there is nothing. No one has any idea what the antecedent is. The deictic designates something, moreover *these* could be rocks, ruins, dreams, anything is possible, something is already, without figure, without body, that has not yet been named. Likewise I was moved to dwell on my mother's *them*. To my question: what do you think of cemeteries? she seemed to have suggested not putting them in a coffin. Cemeteries had just entered the realm of enigma. Only my mother has the key. The use of the coffin was also revolutionized. I was in an anxious mood but my pleasure in sentences always surpasses the project that threatens. My mother has the abrupt genius of a general who disregards so superbly the rules of war and the custom of feigning that he falls with all his might upon the other he's not thinking about and overthrows him without having even tried. A chapter would begin with: "One shouldn't put them in a coffin" if I were my mother. The reader would hesitate. He or she might think that *them* takes the place of shoes, or letters, or that one's talking about a pair of lovers. Or else cats. We were on the edge of the poem, in that undecided expanse between the world and characters of language. We were speaking. During this time my mother attempted some sorties against my macabre extravagance which she finds deplorable.

– Out of the question.

There is nothing to be done.

There is still the undergrowth.

When I see the cemetery, I see the studio of your friend the painter. To live in such an atmosphere disgusts me.

– We don't see each other, I thought to myself, for me cemeteries make up such a part of my interior landscape, I think of them so frequently that I don't notice them any more.

– The cemetery, said my mother, is a catastrophe. People have to get rid of their dead, what do you want? Once you're reduced to nothing. –You believe there is nothing in the Tomb? I say. – Nothing at all, says my mother. After a little while.

To each his or her own believing. The crystal point to which my mother has not the shadow of a believing is almost unthinkable for me. I put faith in this negative experience, or rather in this assurance of nothing because I believe in my mother, but I can barely represent to myself this absolute affirmation without the least shiver of doubt, it is not followed by images, for me, regarding my mother's non-belief I have an absolute non-unbelief, compared to the clarity of her philosophy of nothing at all I am but shadows and stirrings

– One shouldn't put them in a coffin. One should put them in a sheet that's all. I don't see the interest in going to Algiers to remember the dead. You can remember them here.

At that moment I thought I should stay with my mother. On the hypothesis that only the living are living I should give all my time to my mother, or rather I should take all her time, not lose a single drop of it. The idea that she could accomplish the nothing, leave me alone with her Nothing for Everything pierces me. I had so much pain that I stopped believing anything at all, I stopped walking on water, I stopped a few moments, I stopped

My mother circles, she shakes her wings, she lets out several sharp cries. She throws pawn upon pawn as if one could win a game of chess with random moves. She exclaims successively: First of all it's not at all interesting as a country. That doesn't hold up I say. Secondly she says a Jew does not need to go visit the *anti-Semites*, thirdly she says, *which Jew*, I say, *which anti-Semites*? I yelped. Fourthly she says, I've-not-forgotten that they stole my clinic, there's not afffucking thing for me there, you already said that I say, fifthly, that doesn't count I say, I was laughing with anger, sixthly I say, sixthly I didn't go to find the traces of my childhood in Osnabrück, I went because they wanted to ask my forgiveness for what they had done to me, says my mother, that's something I understood, forgiveness doesn't interest you, says my mother, forgiveness is not interesting she says, forgiveness doesn't exist, but when one wants to ask it of you you cannot refuse, all the same says my mother it made no sense, we chatted, we ate well, and no one uttered the word of forgiveness when we were in Osnabrück, I think they forgot. So sixthly? I say

– What kinds of *traces* are you going to find? says my mother. There are no traces.

– The *lycées*, I said feebly.

– Well, if you're interested in the *lycées*.

I spilled a cup of tea on the oilcloth.

There!! Says my mother. *Right here*. She points a powerful finger on the table in front of her plate. Right! here! That means "right here you will wipe the wet sponge!" Right! Here! she says. There's a trace. I see, I say. You don't see, she says. You think I don't know how to wipe a table? I say. –You ought to slow down your activities. It would do you good, says my mother. After all, there is age. – I'm not your age, I say. – Ah! That is true. You see? – I see *what*? You don't see! you don't see anything. – You with your entourage! You are surrounded by a bunch of people who want you to write for them. – You think I should stop writing? – Take care of your steed – Right. Here.

I will always remember I say to myself this long circular joust around the bedeviled dining room table, finally I no longer wanted to go to Algeria, but neither could I give in just at the moment my mother put forward an argument that was arbitrary unjust dangerous senseless historically unfounded philosophically indefensible and into which she breathed all the more sovereign force because she probably didn't believe in it at all. For reasons of pure principle, I could no longer give in, just at the moment when out of love for my mother I wanted to give in, I preferred the love of principle to the love of my mother, a heartrending preference but which I chose precisely out of love for my mother, that is to say out of love for the love for my mother. What truth would this love have had if it were not guaranteed by an absolute spiritual inflexibility

– There! And – there! I wipe the sponge in front of her finger.

– Take your retirement. There! – You mustn't overwork yourself. You and your imaginary friend! It's easier to be the friend of an American who calls on the telephone. – You think I should have a French lover? – There! I like to visit places with sympathetic types.

She strikes, I wipe.

– Wipe!

I wipe.

– What is a tttrace? I was fleeing, I felt my mother's breath on my neck: tttrace! *tttraß!* The word *trace* was mutating, I felt it hissing in a foreign tongue, it became agonizing, monstrous, we had entered swampy country, I was floundering. I interrogated my memory, "what is a trace?" I said, I was ashamed of clinging fast, "Ouch! ouch! ouch!" my memory said, wait! Wait! I have nothing to tell you other than what J.D. told you once and for all, trace, trait, path-breaking. Yes yes I muttered these familiar words, but I rubbed my brain, trace trace trait path-breaking, not the least spark the words hummed and then were erased before I had time for a thought. *Lycées!* chuckled my mother. – The trait, what is the trait? Oh, if only I could go find J.D.!

With humility, confidence, with a mystical hope, without delay, the way one addresses the saving oracle I would ask him – What is a trace? It's about Algeria, I would say. It seems to me, I would say, that I have lost – the meaning. Did I really want to *recover traces*? I said to myself. I was seized by a dreadful doubt: what if one could *not* recover traces? What if, believing for example that I was going to find once again the trees on the squares in Algiers – which is what I "remember" most clearly – what if I went to Algiers the bearer of trees preserved alive for thirty-five years and translated into this mysterious life that is ignited, extinguished, and can be reignited at will in memory, what if this vegetation, at the moment I approached it in reality, disappeared from one second to the next, canceled, erased – replaced by untranslated trees, as devoid of charm as those women fashion models, perfectly beautiful on the outside, who elicit no emotion even though they (the traces) are raised high up on stilted heels. What if one could only lose in reality, and as soon as one approached what one thought was their being they vanished. Myself I was falling apart, I was raving. My mother said: *There's no traces.* She was categorical. – What is a trace!? With what force of annihilation she had struck the word trace with a closed fist. And I had vaguely said: "the *lycées*," while pulling my head down into my shoulders. Myself I was feebly saying feeble words, I was defenseless in face of the assault

And what if there were no traces? Each time round it got worse. I could see very well that I was yielding ground. Moreover I wanted to yield to my mother, but not at any cost. What weakened me was not her strength. The danger after all was not coming from my mother, it was in myself. Everything toward which I turned seemed to shy away.

I had always said "traces, traces", without thinking about it. I liked to caress this word, yet in this instant it was no more than an imaginary horse, you tire yourself out, too much, my mother would say, you waste your time dreaming, if I was dreaming it was of the marvelous sentences with which my friend J.D. might describe, had described, was able to describe, those haughty hills of Algeria those red flanks covered with traces and rising immortally above the massacres and the habitual throat-slittings up to the clouds, I was dreaming of sentences rising up to the clouds with their pointed tips constantly erased by the speed with which they moved, but I no longer remembered the volume in which to find them. My mother's theresnotrace had pierced me through with humility. She has a gift for the crack in the armor I said to myself. She throws words down on the table without looking, without knowing, it's natural, and it never fails they are the most wounding, the most demoralizing

I was seized by that dead-leaf feeling of floating from door to door weightlessly uselessly which grabs hold of me in long confusing dreams. With her right hand my mother was sweeping crumbs off the table, a habit that depicts us, I was a crumb pushed by her wide strong hand to the edge of the board, expelled, thrown over, onto the gray carpet. But I was in reality. At the bottom of my heart, I could not deny it, everything doubts everything. What to expect of the "*lycées*"? As soon as *ly-cée* was cut to pieces by my mother I myself saw nothing more than empty shells. If I had memories – they did not shine at all. I was wandering mentally in the faded, the dull, the hardly visible. In the middle of this disaster there was a cypress. A cypress as visible and as strong as in a dream. Yet it was a *true cypress* that I recognized, a cypress from memory of a rare species: the sparkling visual memory of a unique subject one in a thousand and full of Grace. I see this cypress as I am going down the narrow street that leads from the buildings of the Lycée Fromentin situated on the high esplanade from 1950 to 1954 toward the great gate, just after the hairpin turn, in the curve on the left where a dense and dark vegetation gathers. Low down on the trunk the large sculptural acanthus leaves abound. I feel the humidity of the leaf mould in 2006 I see myself in front of the cypress. I stop a moment. I raise my head. I look for its head. I bend my head back so far it forms a right angle with my shoulders. I finally see the tip of the arrow and then I don't see it any more: the sky begins I abruptly bring my head back to a vertical position so as not to fall over backwards. I come back to earth. The cypress continues. The arrow flies toward my father, whom I locate somewhere in the heights since 1948, at least insofar as he is the face whose gaze follows me, invisibly. The cypress is my mystical postman. I dictate in a half-whisper some words for my father. If the message is to be picked up it must be uttered clearly. And as brief as a prayer. It is not a prayer, it is a greeting. Sometimes I say: good day, my love. And the arrow takes off. Later I will confide the cypress to my beloved, it is one of the first secrets I tell him in 1964, I will see on his face that he is not sure he can recognize a cypress. I will draw it. Slender, willowy, flexible, carried off by a sober exaltation, I see that it is the body of my father. There is no explanation. I do not imagine for an instant that my mother has ever spoken to a tree. Myself, if I wrote about this habit, it would be above all about the different orders of belief: how one believes without believing, without realizing, in silence, how one supports an afterlife on imagined frameworks, how this believing without believing is a believing that resists all resistances, a believing that grows beyond my reason with a sovereign vigor, and for which I am not responsible. How this behavior addressed to invisible images climbs by means of a real, living, concrete support, to see the cypress rising is to find myself at the beginning of the immense road that leads to my father so far away but not so far away, I hold the infinite by one end, I place my hand on its foot. When I ask my mother if she talks to trees, in August 2006, she jerks back and her eyes bulge out, as if she had glimpsed a nightmare face. I sense I am approaching the horrifying for her. I didn't dare tell her my manias until that day. In Algeria I spoke to no one about my literature. I invented half of my events at the *lycées*. but I protected them by a system of lies that made them pass for real. – Or else, I added, toward the sky? – I have nothing to say to it, there is no one behind it. There's no possible response. She spoke to me with an honest firmness, she was trying to convince me to rid myself of the spell. – Those are mo-no-logues. No one has ever done that in the family. Mo-no-logues! She pronounced the word monologue with a triple accent of dismissal.

The mo-no-logue is a solitary activity. In general they are speeches that no one wants to listen to. The mo-no-logue reminds her of a girl who talks non-stop all the more so because she is extraordinarily stupid. Better to keep silent.

61

Does the earth speak? No. The same thing for the air. Skies are different colors of blue. The trees are always there. I observe that this is the case and that's enough.

I observe that there are always seeds in this bread
I am talking to you about the bread.
I prefer the bread from Poilâne.
This bread is from Poilâne that you've been eating for five days
There're no seeds
I don't know if it's from Poilâne
It is from Poilâne. Do you want me to show you the bag?
Yes
She looks at the bag for a long time: "Max Poilâne"
Max Poilâne is another one.
Even when you see you don't believe?
Mine makes bread with holes in it. There're no holes.
There's also the question of the inheritance.
He killed himself in a plane with his wife
Now I don't know who says Max
This bread is another
And you think your Algeria is the same
There is the inheritance
Your father also is another

And my spotted, pale mother, in a bathing suit
Not a wrinkle, the same.

You and your cemeteries
Have you eaten?

"Maman." I say. "Are you going to end up one day mixing bread in with cemeteries?" I thought. I was going to say it I restrained myself. Mixed up myself with bread fear unwillingness, the truth my mother devours my heart. "My beer!" says my mother. I'v'n't finished." She eats the adverbs of negation to save time. At home in Germany one doesn't say no twice, once is enough. *Nicht.* "In the fridge." I go get the beer, now that Algeria has struck Germany is coming back I say to myself.

– The cemetery was already very overgrown. One could hardly get through. I didn't go often. There's nothing one can do there, in the labyrinth. It opens with a little tunnel. One has to crawl through. A few hundred meters. There are lots of objects on the ground, clothes, children's shoes, photo albums. A family has left its things. I don't have the tools to clean it up. I leave.

I give her my arm, I'm afraid she'll fall. Don't go too fast! I say. We are arm in arm in front of the door. All of a sudden she changes sides, she jumps to my side, she says: it's near the back. There is a straight path. All the way up. Take pruning shears. Then to the left near the wall

But at the same time I had jumped to her side, I said: I won't go to Algiers. And we were each of us on the other shore, uprooted, vacillating in the place of the other that the other had just at that moment left so as to be on the same side

– All those *People* who surround you, they want you to write, said my mother who has always been mistaken in forgiving my unforgivable need to write by means of the obscure divine figure of "People," my mother can't believe that her daughter is the sole author of her madness, she prefers to think that I am the slave of "People" rather than the slave of my own choice, and since only the gods could lead into crime a daughter and a mother – which I am badly – to the gods my mother lends the human faces of "People" among whom jostle Yourfriends, Yourpublisher, and Yourflatterers. They want you to write *Youreturn to Algeria.* But these powers she wrongly attributes to "People," it is my mother who had them

63

in reality, her words called up in me an indisputable marvel, I
had the vision of a grotesque colloquium the subject of which
is Return to Algiers, I am stuck among some "People," I am
on the verge of weeping alas weeping is impossible I would
have to have a little interior life, upon seeing the crowded
colloquium my tears flee, I cannot get up at all, I want to go
away, be moved, I saw this colloquium coming, instead of
Algiers the colloquium, if Algiers was going to lead me to a
colloquium instead of leading me through the zones of inde-
termination of my interior life, I would not go

I will not go further, I say to myself, so I will not go to
Algiers. Or else I will not write. Or else I will write that I
did not go to Algiers. After all one can't cook up one's life.
I couldn't any longer want to go to Algiers. I was afraid of
eating Algiers.

I had to approve of Zohra. She didn't call. She will not call,
I thought. And naturally she didn't call. She didn't call me. I
had such a high and radiant idea of what "Algiers" must be if
I went there not to rediscover things of the past but to discover things that had never happened there, that could never
have happened when I lived there but could only be produced
with the unique violence of the unique time. I wanted to go
to the Jardin d'Essai with J.D., in reality, in a conjunction of
realities with the Jardin d'Essai, of which I have often written as he has written more than once like me. When I wrote
"We are from the same garden" he wrote "we are from the
garden itself" I write my Jardin d'Essai, he writes "the Jardin
d'Essai is situated near a soccer field where I often went to
play" but not me. "This garden still exists," he wrote that in
2004, without *knowing* if the Garden still existed, but out of
certainty and belief, thinking without thinking that the Jardin
must stillexist. We have never been there together in real
reality, but with time, in time, with the future, we have been
there dozens of times. By dint of citing it and describing it,

we have brought it to the mythological summit. From now on "This Garden still exists" exists for eternity in the volume of J.D.'s works. Everyone may believe from now on, especially in the USA or in Japan, where critical culture willingly hesitates between theology and poetics, that the "Jardin d'Essai" is a fiction, whereas the Jardin d'Essai *is* a *natural* fiction. It is the Dream of the Most Beautiful Garden in the World. "We never went there together, but it represents a kind of lost paradise" he wrote. Thus, if I went to Algiers, the first thing I wanted to do with J.D. was naturally to see in reality the true Jardin d'Essai, so as to discover, with time having done its work on its side, how the Jardin d'Essai still exists lost. No one could not love the Garden of the Jardin d'Essai, it was not a permitted Garden, it was what remained of the Lost Paradise that remembered it and recalled continuously to the faithful the unimaginable splendor of what is lost.

I wanted to go to Lycée Fromentin with Zohra Drif, with whom I had been in the same class for the final four years there, without ever once having had the chance to tell her what I was thinking and that I was thinking about what she was thinking during French classes. Especially when we were studying *The Song of Roland*, which I detested adoring, I turned around in order to try to see Zohra Drif's expression, if it was still the same. It was still the same. My agitation was solitary, head down, frowning, inscrutable, Zohra, like a sealed letter. I detested adoring but I did not like detesting adoring, I did not like the mental complication I felt as soon as I entered those narrow passes I felt accused and I was guilty, yes I was, I felt it, I was guilty of those meanders, those obscurities, those divisions, that subterraneity which enveloped me in the middle of class, that cry of disavowal which I did not cry aloud and which turned back round on me in me. And what lived in me, attached like my dog to its leash, was the misery of this reversed protest, this semi-protest, raised and then aborted, it was the horror of this turning back round that broke my momentum and made me fall back on myself constantly in the opposite sense. I valued above all the idea of fidelity that I inherited from my father and I found that it was totally inaccessible to me, I loved Roland and suddenly I no longer saw any way to love him, I left him, later I began to love him again but dying and cared for by my father the lieutenant doctor but dead and beyond Catholicism. What is Zohra Drif going to think? I used to ask myself. I could neither give up reading *The Song of Roland*, nor embrace Catholicism, nor accept the conditions on reading *The Song*, I began to read passionately, faithfully, up to the moment when I couldn't any longer, I pulled myself out of the fidelity parade, I did a pirate reading, I drew *The Song* toward me but who was I, I did several different readings at the same time when I rebelled with the Saracens I was nevertheless on the side of laughter and thus of Roland, I couldn't sleep, I went to bed right before the battle I read I turned from one side to the other, before the corpse of the one I could understand Count Roland's pain I could understand the pain of King Malcud before the other corpse, before each corpse the same pain in the streaming air the detestable words of detestation dirty race may God send every curse upon you and with such vigor that he splits his helmet down to the noseguard slices his nose his mouth his teeth his whole chest at the same time as his coat of mail the two silver humps of his golden saddle and deep into the spine of the horse he kills them both and without any possible recourse the knight the horse and deeply god, but the song has no tears except on one side, *dieu est coupé en dieux*, god is cut into two gods, each god for himself, may god not help you, in front of each stanza I could understand the color of the song when I saw that the song sees Count Roland as more and more white the others as more and more black and having only teeth that are white I can do

66

nothing but throw the book across the room it falls under the chair. It's quite useless. I am touched on all sides, no blood that is not mine all bloods flow human, I cannot prevent the bloods from flowing over the eyes of all those whose names are gathered either in one color or under the opposite color the bloods are absolutely the same the song is so beautiful it behaves ignominiously, all these brave men are equal in cruelties and communities, I can no longer close my eyes I saw the other killed, all kill the others, all the others of the others kill the others all smother trust and pity, the spine of the gods split without possible recourse, pride and wrongdoing are on all sides. But the very subtle and passionate song pours all the portions of tears over the one to whom it has sworn fidelity. All of a sudden I recognize its incense and fusional blandishment. How is evil beautiful, how beautiful evil is, and how seductive is dreadful pride, I am terrified. I have loved evil, pain, hurt, I hate it, all of a sudden I hatedloved it. The song seduced and abandoned me. No, I abandoned myself to the song. There is no greater treachery

What pained me was the rumor, the executioner was coming any second now for the victim, every other stanza I saw myself as the enemy of my friends and vice versa I loved the friends who did not love me I dreamt that I was on the good side I woke up on the other, my friends my enemies in truth, I maintained a wounded fidelity, a wound, an infidelity opened up within fidelity, from Roncevaux I arrived in Algiers, it was just one step from the song to the *lycée* it is just one wound which caused me even more pain than the thing that pained me, this betrayal that I caused myself and against which I could not defend myself was the fact that I said to myself: what else worrisome is there in addition behind the brawling, and especially behind Z.D.'s frown, what reading, which I don't know, which I don't see, which I will never know? This unknown zone that began very close by so far away, where I glimpsed at the back of the class the hazy blond of Z.D.'s hair, took on an unlimited magnitude. The song sings its treacherous hymn to treachery, I don't know what she hears. A river runs through the classroom. I kill you because you were born on that shore over there. But what pains me even more is the powerlessness that takes up all the space between my desk on the left and Z.'s desk in back on the right. The idea that I might take advantage of a recess to talk to Z.D. about *The Song of Roland*, first prudently, from the stylistic point of view, then suddenly to reveal myself, but what? who? how? in which language? To go to the end of a sentence I would have to traverse North Africa, Rome, France, Spain, the empires of the Orient and the Occident and the legacies of beliefs in the belongings to peoples, religions, races, histories, nations, rights, and on top of it all literature, ever since its invention up until the French course at the Lycée Fromentin where *The Song of Roland was taught* by applying the rules of scholastic hygiene. Moreover I knew absolutely nothing about Z.D. All my ambitious constructions were built on her lowered eyelids. It may be that I began to recognize in myself the hypothesis that nothing could ever undo the Fromentin fate: all was lost in advance, I thought, by the mandatory corruption, the condition for entry into the *lycée*, a French establishment for the French. It had been understood that we were at Fromentin as what we were not, neither one of us. I had seen my father worried by the French purity of Fromentin just before his death. It was not forbidden to be impure at Fromentin, that is to say, improperly French, provided one didn't say so. One was not, one did. One thought to the side and from beneath. Head-on one did the French girl. Nothing ought to let anyone suspect we were not sincerely converted. Who can tell the powers of conversion? One can believe one believes to the point of managing to be. Without the lowered gaze of Z.D., without a reservation in her voice,

68

which I interpreted as symptoms of a retrenchment (without my compulsion for deciphering all the signs of all the bodies and all the faces in the book of my entourage), except for a pout where I thought I saw a bridle bit, but it dissipated, perhaps I would not have begun to live Algeria on hypotheses. Besides that would have changed nothing in my will, I wanted to leave the class to begin to leave Algeria, at the Lycée I could stay seated at my desk only because I trusted in my will to leave, I was not in Algiers, I still remained, not once in my final year did I have the least image of a second part of my life that would find me in a street of Algiers, I wanted to be done with the legacy of betrayal that had come down to me only by mistake and misunderstanding, with the immobile force of fate I moved toward the exit, at the end of the street take the vast staircase then the arcade to the right where the second part begins.

I never gave Z.D. any sign at the Lycée Fromentin she never gave me any sign. I could only approve of her. I say to myself. Later I had the pointless desire to write to Zohra I say to myself. The enormity of destinerrancy diverted me from it. It would have been a letter without any chance and without any risk of going beyond my reverie. I held onto the idea. It might have evaporated. It was moreover the shadow of an idea.

Years later I did not write a letter to Zohra Drif. I abruptly wrote the "Letter to Zohra Drif."

– I have no reason to go to Algeria, I say to myself.
– Maybe I have a third bathing suit! says my mother. "A two-piece." Her look consults mine. "Go ahead" I say. The bathing suits come back. My mother's delighted intimidated expression. "May I?" she says. A marvelous youth bubbles up in her mind. Why not? Everything is marvelously possible,

69

bodies follow the bathing suits, my mother returns, I had totally forgotten her, myself I had consented to the militant orders of time, I no longer thought about the former divinity of my mother, the memory doesn't interest me. A German bathing suit, says my mother, I bought it at the market for a song. The greatest illusion is to think that what is passed is finished, I say to myself. It's a two-piece bathing suit. At that moment I did something unbelievable. The idea of filming my mother leaped to my heart, and this madness of immortality, I committed it. I said: "I am going to film you." My mother said nothing. I ran up to get the movie camera, which is not mine. I have no movie camera. I have never had a movie camera in my whole life I have never taken a photo, I have never taken anything, I have pushed "you shall make for yourself no graven image" to the height of extremes, I have never taken a photo of my beloved, there are no photos of our life, not a single image, I did not take photos of my children, I did not take my brother, or my women friends, or my friend J.D. I never fought off a desire to photograph or to film, I never had the sudden urge to keep a visual trace, I should have perhaps sometimes I will never know if I did the wrong thing I can't I can no longer look back it's too late. There was a movie camera in my study, the one that my friend Ruth Beckermann had left with me the day I said to her: I will perhaps go to Algiers. My friend the Viennese film-maker went back to Vienna, saying to me: if you go to Algiers, film. If I go to Algiers, I will not film I say to myself, if there is one occasion on which I will not film it is Algiers, I have never filmed anyone in my life. I have never touched a movie camera. I have never put an apparatus for looking between desired subjects and the retinas of my soul. Without explanation. I came running back down. My mother was already in her film. In the film in which she is the subject, the cause. There was no question in front of her. Not a word between

70

the announcement "I am going to film you" and my entrance with the camera. My mother is in a state of supernatural consent. Is that possible? I don't believe so. The idea occurs to me that perhaps it's not she who obeys, but I who am obeying a will external to my will which has taken over my will by a trick, it may be that it's my mother's will, hidden to herself or on the contrary hidden by herself, silent, powerful, of unquestionable authority, which dictated to me this abrupt and crazy decision: to film my mother in a purple two-piece. I filmed. What did I film? My mother's will. I thought: Maman's will and testament. Back up a little, I say. I don't know how to see my whole mother in the little screen. Come closer? Back up? Who? Back up, I say. Another step. Now: I see my mother. It is the first time. I see and I see that I see. I see my mother in painting. I see what I have as yet never seen what I will never

see. I take the camera and I paint my mother with large brush strokes, I have never seen my mother I say to myself I have never seen her so close, I see my mother in a two-piece, I paint the body from top to bottom, then from bottom to top, I invent my mother from all sides, turn around, there is a pale blue note below, the slippers I paint the slippers, tableau: *the pale blue slippers*, they have a life, and more than one, a proper life and an other life, when I paint them in the continuation of the barely dressed body in the purple two-piece bathing suit, *my mother with blue slippers*, take off the slippers, she removes the slippers, *my mother without slippers*, the calmest feet I have ever known, render the calm of the feet, the firmness of the big toes, that's the secret, the strength in the big toes, I say: "it's beautiful." I say: turn around and go toward the window. I repeat. She doesn't hear. I repeat. She goes toward the window, I paint the slightly stooped shoulders, the confident step. I don't know what we know, or how she knows, but I know that we know. I think: it's a masterpiece. I don't know what it is but I'm sure of it. The beauty of my mother's beauty

71

in a bathing suit, the matchless work of my mother, the glory of the body stronger than time, a drawing whose depth surpasses the gullies of the epidermis, what is that called, when is made visible the invincible radiance of a body that has made the trip, with soul intact, without rust, without ruin, without crack, content? My mother describing herself, self-portrait of the artist with camera, I was only contemplating. "My mother as simple immortal," I say to myself. Or else "My mother in two-piece in All Simplicity." She is on her own side.

As for me, if I go to one side, I see myself from the other side. Even on the subject of Algeria, my mother is now entirely on one side, now entirely against, even for Israel either she is totally for the policies of the government, or else totally against. She has not known torment. Whereas I have not known simplicity. If the world is square I am on the four sides. The number four creates me with complications, I was born by four roads, I always and never have the choice of choosing or not where to be me, where to put my thoughts, my notebooks, my hopes, imagine a heart cut into four quarters in a body that is all the same obliged to settle itself as a single being. I advance by fours, unequally, I have four mouths with which to say I at the same time, without counting the unconscious that speaks I by the hundreds on my face, and that externally is indistinguishable from my skin, this fatal paste of words piled, mixed, spread like poison on my psychic life, these dreadful occult adjectives whose meanings I don't know in the least but whose violently ruinous effects I see everywhere, all of them, for the most part, registered around the worse word, the word Jew, the wordjew the worsejew, a paste of chewed-up words spit upon the being, who passes for me, who passes in the street, in the crowd, in the city, being all the time under distortion doesn't facilitate movement. Especially since I don't have the answer that I am asked, even I don't know what I'm saying when I don't deny and don't affirm but confirm being

72

in indistinction part Sephardi part Ashkenazi part Jewish still another Arab, another part Germanic, all these parts that partition my cells how do they geograph my being where does one part begin where does it continue stop melt dash trample, my hand, there, this one, that in this moment is groping in the psychic brambles of my tattoos, is it the seph- or ash-index with ash- or seph-thumb with sephash or ashseph fingers up to what point, for how long, and then the nails and the lines, the famous lines that message the totality of our destiny, we have being in the hand, but we don't know how to read ourselves, my point of view is buried in my hand not counting the famous lines of the mongoloid's hand those of my son of another species that he left inscribed in my hand

Whereas my mother says "our home" and one sees that it's Germany, even in Algeria still more in France, whereas I have never been able to say "your home," or else I say in Al- and that's all I can't land on more than one syllable, I don't even try, every ground retreats under my feet, I have frontiers everywhere in the verb to be, the red paint is yellow on my forehead, no says Yes when I am questioned, or yesbut or nobut, yesnobut sephardi-butashkenazi, sepharashkenazardi here and there otherwise anagram. I realize wherever I want wherever I go in all good faith all of a sudden I am but. If I *am* somewhere, it is at fault. Wipe, says my mother. I am wiped out. I confess that I am born-but, it's when it's my fault that is not mine. I am all mixed up with but.

I will complete this with what I noted in the Hugo Notebook about the *affair of the croissants*, which illustrates the extraordinary way in which I am politically persecuted in my acts and gestures because of my original complication. Then I will end up by calling Zohra in Algiers:

On July 27 I take *the last* train for Paris, that is to say my mother, relieved to be done with all these colloquia that is

73

to say these questionings, it's in the train that I understand nebulously from some words in the air because no one addresses me directly, that this convoy is not going to Paris where I saw myself arriving saved in a few hours, but will not stop before arriving at the other end of the country in the last station before the end. From there one has to find a train that goes back in the opposite direction toward Paris. During the very long trip I see my whole life roll by, naturally I think constantly about the end about death, about the urgency of finding my mother again and the cats who will die if deprived of me, that is, may my fragile dear ones find me again but I can do nothing. Several times I think I recognize passengers, they are persons I have met but with whom I have never spoken, by reason of colloquia, those places where people speak but not with each other, I follow them with my eyes, they don't show the least sign, which means: "Jew." It was like that in Algeria all those cut-off signs, that always meant "Jew." The eyes as well. People who have eyes on command. I see a man pass whom I have already seen, an athletic blond, finally it's a woman. I fall asleep from fatigue and I dream that I am sitting with my mother and my brother at the extreme end of a bench there is so little room that I am sitting on the ground in my place. After all I say to myself one needs nothing more to live than the earth. It's when the train is a boat that I find the interminable crossing intolerable. I had something with the earth that limited the abyss. If the train is a boat I'm worried. I decide to ask for some information. I cross the boat, which is enormous, one of those Cities with classes underclasses decks underdecks, hell afloat, a summing up of the state of social war that makes for all the dead under the stairs. I finally arrive on the deck of the superiors where there is naturally The Pool. And I see those-ladies-who-pull-long-faces-at me. I should write a book about this. I move closer all the same. Each time I come closer all the same. The closer I come the more they talk with one another. I address them. They talk with one another as if my name were Merzouka, although my name is not Merzouka. This is all part of the hostility of acting as if there were a mistake. I know they are hostile to me. The world is full of these ladies of hostility. They know that I am not a disease but they act as if they might catch me. There is always one who says: Cixous what kind of country is that? I answer: it's German. When I was young I used to say naïvely: it's Kabyle-Jewish. Now I ask them why we are not stopping in Paris. One of the women moves away and goes all tight-lipped. One of the women finally answers me reticently. She is in the water that is the sea itself infinite, in which are swimming cats and dogs the size of thimbles. She tells me the truth. No one knows if we are going to arrive. What?! She says to me: do you hear? The hull of the City is cracking. It's a matter of hours. I am stunned. We're going to sink? In a little while. Bitter I say to myself that if I hadn't crossed the first line of the front I would not even have known that we were going to the end of the world, these ladies would have taken my death from me. What to do? The boat is under discussion the lady informs me. Dispute with the American government. They might come rescue us in a helicopter. It's far this sea and one wastes time with governments. The ladies in the know have retained a lawyer. But I have friends, I say. I have a lawyer friend. We're on the same boat after all. This notion makes them laugh. I feel doubly impotent, from the situation and from the hostility. The tight-lipped one makes a terrible face at me. Apparently she hates me even more for having deprived her of a delicious little satisfaction: if she had succeeded, I would have sunk in an altogether other way. So I attempt a sortie: "this is not the moment to have antipathies," I say. When there is war, on principle I don't let go, I go all the way toward peace. Especially if it is once again the end of the world. When there is nothing more to be done, there is no more earth, there is the sea, there is no more sea, there is shipwreck, me, I am always looking for a thimbleful of reason in the ocean. "What is the cause?" I say. I'm addressing myself to the worst one. The tight-lipped lady says: "*The croissants.*" The croissants!? What an answer. So there is a cause. Two minutes ago I had the hope of exposing injustice. Now I was checkmated. The end. Guilty. A dumbfounded culpability grabbed hold of me. How to reject such an extraordinary accusation. So unexpected. So precise. The croissants are against me. I remain unable to speak. I don't dare deny. Had I taken too many croissants? Last week? In a gathering? In the past? Slow heavy anxiety about the obscure transgression grows rises in my veins besieges my head. An affair of croissants can easily lead to hatred. And consequently from hatred to hatred all the way to Destruction. Wars, massacres, begin exactly like that. I am aware of it. Between the hostile ones and me there is *interpretation*. So it is hopeless. Someone says: "The croissants." It's understood there are too many, that is to say not enough. I confess that I love croissants. Obscurely, I feel the power of the "croissants" swelling. Had I been spied on? Did someone denounce me? I ask myself for an explanation. Perhaps the croissants were the property of these ladies? Perhaps I abused them immeasurably? A glance at the judges. I recognize them. These ladies look very French. Guilty of very French croissants, I say to myself, I had never thought of that. I ate croissants without thinking about it, even as we live in the world that is the most mistrustful of History, the most policed, the most nationalist, I was eating croissants croissants I believed absorbed in the butter and puff pastry. What am I saying! Did I ever even imagine for a moment that a person without cross was not welcome to devour *croixsang*, cross-bloods? I was eating pastries, I believed! These croissants must have the dignity, status, meaning of the communion wafer for these ladies to bear me a mortal grudge.

every five minutes blood is spilled in the world over a problem of croissant or sans-cross, which at one end touches on
the ridiculous at the other end on the tragic. It's at that point
that the croissant idea was specified even further. The prob-
lems of the breakfast croissant is one thing. The croissant or
crescent of Islam is another thing. One crescent increases the
other. Guilty of *croissant* and guilty of *sans-cross*, both at once.
Innocence is not what you think. To be sure the thought of
Algiers stays with me. But never in my life have I made Islam
stand for Algeria, but neither can I imagine Algiers without
its crescents, that's natural. So "The croissants," aggressively
pronounced, and without explanation, like a capital punish-
ment, was the set of croissants/crescents I had abused, an
inadmissible condensation of opposites. Arguing is pointless.
So "the croissants" will have been the last word of my story. I
move away. I find this ending too oppressive and frightening.
Such an urge to confide my dismay. Is there anyone to talk
to? Is there a chance of survival? I think of calling my mother.
And not saying anything to her. She will spend the last hours
without worry. I'm certainly not going to tell her this petty
story of the verbal croissant. I call her. I say: Maman. She says:
mydaughter! I say: I love you. She says: this is going to cost
you dear. Quickly I say again: Maman. I don't want to end with
dear. If we sink I say to myself all will have ended on ma-, since
my mother had hung up. I had just enough time. If I come out
of it – which depends on the dispute with the American government – I will be able to recount what happened right when
I was writing my impossible book on Algeria.

A totally white, blank notebook. I note: *States before-
Algiers*. I cross out. Nothing is yet decided. I note: Torn by
a thousand ties I'm drawn and quartered. I note: the White
Notebook (1) for everything I don't know and (2) for every-
thing that might have been, could be, could not be; the Victor
Hugo Notebook for Z. Be careful while in Paris where I put

the wrenching sentences don't put the moments of sentences dictated by Algiers. If ever I go to Algiers it will be another notebook. We'll see.

In a book I would write how almost everything urges me not to go to Algiers. Thus at the end of the chapter, suddenly, I would go. But I was in reality

When I returned to Algiers in reality that is to say every year from 1955 until 1971, I went back to my mother's, I lived at the Clinic on the Rue d'Isly first then the Rue Ben M'hidi Larbi, I had just come to leave Algiers again, I did not just come to come back to Algiers but to my mother's, I thought I would come back leave again every year until the end, until the day in the year 1971 when my mother was kicked out of Algiers in the course of one day, I had always thought she would finish out her life in Algiers during all those years I never went back to the Lycée Fromentin. I never went to the Lycée Bugeaud, I could have gone to the Cemetery where I never went, I went once to Clos-Salembier where our childhood home had disappeared, I could have gone to Algiers dozens of times, I never thought of it in reality.

Zohra did not call, I expected it, it's hypernatural I said. The unexpected is that she "responded" years and years later, she hadn't called moreover, that was impossible, she had someone call me, and I wasn't there, as one might expect in my mythology calls are diverted into gorges they never arrive except in the form of third-person narratives I said, they have wandered so long among the rocks that they can no longer find their object in reality, I said that to F., for her this made no sense, she was disappointed, she found it to be a dreadful thing, someone says they want to call and they don't call, she complained about Z.'s silence but it was mine that she blamed like an obscure, bizarre fault. Now I was on Z.'s side, not F.s side. According to me. The way in which Z. makes her way toward me symmetrically to my making my way toward her,

78

with the immense and fragile freedom of persons who are in the quietude of nothingness and who do not know what awaits them at the exit from such a long nothing, is familiar to me. I can only approve of myself I thought. I too, I didn't call. If she didn't call after the "at-all-costs" message, it's because the causes of the non-call had won out. I could imagine dozens of them. On both sides. After all there had never been a single conversation between Z. and H. Years spent on the same French ocean liner, to be sure there is a metonymy but that doesn't interest me. Not that she hadn't called me in 1952, then in 1953, while responding in advance to my call that had been muted by the anxiety and rage of not seeing any exit ex-Algeria at the Lycée Fromentin, not that she didn't respond to me before having herself found the response herself not that she was not already in response to my enraged fear of never finding an exit, which drove me to leave all those *lycées* with French locks paradoxically without any other possibility of extracting myself from that fate except by moving toward the only unblocked direction for someone of my kind kicked out of all countries including the expelling ones, France Germany Austria Hungary Bulgaria Romania, not that she didn't respond to me point by point, and of the class's whole face I had retained only the frown, the knitted brow on the shutters. And also the trick of blonde hair to mislead onto the wrong French trail.

Now, however, we have something in common I said to myself. Since the phone call, Z . and H. keep the same silence. So I telephoned. I said: Zohra? And the voice said: No. Wait a second. I say: *Huc Coeamus* – And it's over. From one second to the next. We speak to each other. The book in which we had never managed to speak to each other is finished. Ended. Here. We will never again be able to make not happen this end that flees. Already a beginning has been thrown so quickly into the place left empty by the end that the two characters

Z. and H. are overtaken, the next beginning rushes on. And what if I had not telephoned? One must sometimes choose between the time of hearing and the time of speaking.

Why now? I said to Zohra. Decades, one thing and another, never anything decided last year all of a sudden decided, all the same, thought: find H.C., dozens of times, one thing another thing, but, all those friends who told me read the text by H.C., it's about a letter, I read your letter to Z.D. in English, you know my English she says, I don't know I say, I was not very good at the *lycée* you know, it's extraordinary, life, you know this race, I know I say, frantic race she says, last year all of a sudden must absolutely find H.C. why now, it's time, so the message is sent "find at all costs," now she has the number, the dates. She says it's extraordinary. I've wanted to call you for a month. Every day I say to myself I am going to call her. Finally I didn't do it. I don't know why. Now Z. has the number. So, she doesn't call I thought on my side. So. I note. I pick up the Victor Hugo notebook. I write Z. on the cover. Next to the tower drawn by Victor Hugo. Now I think: Hugo, Fromentin, Zohra, Hélène, a hundred pages, to come. I note: H. notes: Z. doesn't call. So H. doesn't call. One day H. says: Today I will call Z. She calls Algiers. Zohra speaks. It's Zohra. She says it's extraordinary. I agree: it's extraordinary. What? This, this interminable phantom communication, this conversation that doesn't take place, that doesn't take place, that doesn't take place, that doesn't take place. Until the day *it starts up again*. She says: I said to Samia. I think: thus still together. I think: 1952 in 2005. I think: she says Samia naturally. She says: "I said to Samia." As if forgetting did not exist. As if it were possible not to forget. The idea that I might have forgotten Samia does not occur to her, the idea that I might have forgotten her as I've forgotten hundreds of students from

80

the *lycée* and as I've forgotten fifty or so professors from the *lycée*, afterwards I have forgotten by the hundreds, every year I forget a hundred or so people, the idea occurs to me that the idea does not occur to Z. that I might forget. I can only recognize that she is right: I have not forgotten Samia. She says: "it's *fantastic*" in three words. The fantastic word comes back. I had not tasted it since Algiers, it's an acidulated word, a word of sheer ice like those whose rosy granita Albertine makes melt in the back of her throat, it's a nymph, I had forgotten her in a fountain under the plane trees. I say "fantastic!" and I'm thirteen years old and Zohra has a green-checked smock. Samia gets undressed nonchalantly, gathers herself, runs with delicate speed, as if the thrill of the race resided in an art of not touching it, falls back into nonchalance at the end of the track. The lower lip puffed out. A fugitive in flower. "Fantastic!"

"*Selecto*" says J.D. Why have I not forgotten Samia? I have even forgotten friends, those close to me, beings with whom I traveled, played, slept. All my life is a battle between what I forget what I do not want to forget, what I want to forget, what I shelter, what I unforget, what I fight to pull from the mouth of death, which I tear from its jaws, I spend my whole life in front of those jaws, my hands in those jaws. Or else, I say to myself suddenly, I would never have been able to forget them, neither Zohra, nor Samia, nor the set of the two friends, because without anyone ever knowing it at Fromentin, they were already characters in a book that would be written later, and I saw them perhaps like the living versions of those two women promised to the strange authority of written things. But forgetting does not happen on command. It remains for a long time asleep rolled up in its own fold of forgetting, inactive, distracted. Then oxidation begins. Nothing in the world, no one, will ever escape effacement

Fantastic! I say again. Forty? asks Z. I respond: forty-five. We don't say fifty, that's too much, that's incredible. It's not

Without

fifty. It is still more fantastic. Fifty-two years is how long the Without has lasted, perhaps fifty-three. A separation without separation, an arrest, without example, a sort of borderless strait of time between two worlds, a sort of intermittent telepathy, or intermittence by telepathy, a vast limitless zone where graze phantoms, vague possibilities, silhouettes of blind mutes, somewhere on this expanse of continual silence I once inscribed a name. Not a sound. Memory continues to tell no one its little stories, forgetting awaits its hour. What is frightening for the lion is the patience of the python: forgetting does not leap on the lion. It begins by mentally swallowing the strong living beast. This virtual ingestion that goes on right up to the last second is perfectly real. The lion's whole soul goes down little by little into the belly. Just a little more and nothing will have ever existed. That's when I cut off. I interrupted the slow process of nothingness. Why now? I interrupted. The python had just coiled up its fifty-second circle of himself. I couldn't do otherwise: I picked up the telephone. I cut death off. I could have waited two more years but it was impossible.

– I am perhaps going to go to Algiers, I say. Now I had to say it. I could now no longer go to Algiers without telling Zohra, as politeness required. She says: I am soon going to be coming through Paris. You'll call me then I say. She says: it's fantastic and I: yes fantastic, I say. "As soon as you arrive, we'll see each other" I was saying. I see you I was saying. That's because French uses a present for a future. In French I saw myself seeing without seeing Zohra whom I hadn't seen in decades. I see her as soon as she arrives. Because of this present that spreads its magic on the future, I think I already see her and that I will see her.

Why now?

I gave my mother a book so she could cut its pages. *Learning to Live Finally* she reads. That's the title. Why now? Did he think he had to do things quickly? – I don't know. – Maybe I should read it some day, says my mother. – Why not now? She reads, she holds the book down beneath her two hands her nails polished pink this morning. Her face follows the pages rises slowly moves slowly from left to right. Portrait of my mother reading *Learning to Live Finally*. Titmice whistle in the oak. My brother asks: what are those red flowers there were some in Algeria. – Geraniums, I say. A squirrel crosses the tree top chirping why why. My mother now holds the book firmly by the shoulders, her hands wide. All of a sudden she thinks of the nurses condemned to death in Libya. I ask myself why I gave my mother this book to cut now. Now she has both hands joined on the belly of the book. She places the right hand with the large ring on the right-hand page. When she extends the left hand over the left-hand page I see that the hand is the size of the page. She sets down her left wrist. She reads calmly without effort. She says "It's interesting, it's good. I'm stopping. I'm not going to read it all now." She says: "In Algiers, the best fish, when you go to the Admiralty, is the restaurant La Pêcherie".

– I will call you, I say. When I am at La Pêcherie. I will tell you the menu.

The idea of telephoning Algeria to my mother as one telephones beyond. To the beyond. The way my beloved telephones New York to me. But I never dared to suggest this trick to my mother. She believes only in touching. She reads while pressing the palms of her hands on the body of the book. We have just taken the first step into the beyond, my mother and I. I am sadly delighted.

What journeys we make! I say to myself. A journey hidden in the journey.

Oh! this plane, already it was Algeria I was thinking, and I had a dizzy spell, as if the urgency of finally arriving had shattered my senses, this last hour this nowhere, this plane, were for me the unlivable, I stopped living, and became conscious again when the plane must have been on the ground for some undetermined length of time, since there was no longer anyone on board, except for me. The long, empty, mortuary machine. In front of me on the tray table my mess of papers. No doubt I had been writing when the cut-off happened. I hastily began gathering up the sheets of paper, shot through with the apprehension that airports cause me. How many times I've been detained by the police, interrogated, interpellated incarcerated. I imagine the terrible passage, the quarrels, the customs agents, the judges, waiting for me as soon as I get off the plane to the right I'm trembling I can't go any faster or perhaps any slower all these papers are likewise defending themselves, fearful, reticent. Everything is getting worse as usual. In the end I will exit, it's unavoidable. But thereupon, in the cabin of the dream, there are two policemen in shirt sleeves, they approach, go past me. I'm not the one they're after? I immobilize myself, I'm no longer breathing. And yet there is no one other than me in this plane. In front, the two men bend over some deserted seats and pick up a piece of trash. It's a madwoman. A woman bent in two who cries: I am dead. The porters do the removal. The body cries: I am dead. Poor madwoman. Suddenly the cortege slows down in front of me. No, no I say hurriedly, I am not mad, I am a writer. With a vague frightened gesture, I point to the proof that this madness of papers is the appearance of a writer. I am dead says the other. And I: no, no, believe me, I am a writer! What an arrival!

85

With this dream as prophet, I go to the airport. Whether I was mad, dead, or a writer, I felt that there would be no more *enemy* life for me until I had seen it again, that there would be no more peace for me after I had seen it again, that this journey would become something fatal, that the immense losses awaiting me, especially mental losses, concerning which I had not the least idea, merely the terror, would probably be everything I fear desiring the most in the world that is to say madness. And that if I had clashed so much with my mother for saying no to me until now this quarrel had been merely a chance to which I clung of not going to Algeria, without losing my unconscious face.

The planes began taking off the scales from my eyes. They landed in my dreams with the grace of a serpent. Hissed: "Algeria." Each day and now each night brought me closer to Algeria. My mother had let me go. She already saw me at La Pêcherie. I could no longer stop sliding toward the end

This year I was thinking all the time of Albertine, I was fascinated by this fleeting, multiplying thing, I wondered why I went back sometimes to the prisoner sometimes to the apparition sometimes to the vanished one, sometimes to the revenant, I was swinging like a monkey from her branches, I passed along her corridors that began to resemble my corridors, her closed doors my doors, when I stopped prowling in place I thought right away of Algeria, at first I had thought that I was clinging to Albertine so as not to think all the time about Algeria, but one evening when speaking to my daughter about *my albertinage* I wanted to excuse or accuse my obsessive penchant for fiction, I make a slip. With a ridiculous sinking feeling in my soul I realize that my passion for Albertine is because of her quasi-homonymy with Algeria. I thought I was distracting myself from Algeria with Albertine. One is ignorant of what one knows, that I know it doesn't prevent me from not knowing it. One story at the same time

86

tells another story says my daughter to console me. But which one is telling which? – One doesn't know. That's why it is a modern allegory. All the same in my case, that is, in my Algeria passion the end remains unforeseeable.

In the white notebook I note: "*To return*" one doesn't know what it is: *to come back to before*. Keyed up at the idea of "returning" thus of turning myself back, of being turned round, turned inside out (in the opposite sense – but which one? I am already "returned" in the two opposite senses) of being returned (to sender, unknown at the Algeria address) of being turned round (against my benefactors to whom I owe everything, which ones?)

Every day I come closer to the fated necessity of Algeria. One surrenders to fate without knowing its features. But you recognize it by the force of irresistible attraction that emanates from a square opening cut out two meters up in the thickness of the wall that closes off the horizon of the world's attic. The height of the hole is calculated: from far away one can see nothing. Up close one must stand on tiptoe or raise oneself up enough by perching on a book in order to respond to the pressure of curiosity. I cross the room cluttered with vestiges. In front of me a cat scoots by with gold fur striped in shining black. She's holding in her mouth her small copy, her golden refuse. She too is dashing toward the opening as toward salvation. The allegory is beyond question. When after crossing through memory I reach the unknown into which the cat has disappeared, I hoist myself up to the window frame. The slit in the wall that leads to the other world is dirty, poorly maintained, covered with rough spots. Only the force of irresistible attraction drags me into taking a risk because left to my own impulse I would recoil. And I see.

What awaits me, immobile, immense, inevitable, its head vast as the future occupying all visible space, like a star filling up totally the earth's orifice, a lion, in truth: *The Lion*. The whole cat and company are already under his charm. I had totally forgotten the lion of 54 Rue Philippe in Oran. One approached the door on which he reigned. One grabbed hold of him by his bronze mane, one knocked two sharp blows for Cixous and my grandmother appeared in response to the lion on the balcony. Seen from anxiety and desire, from the anxiety of desiring so much, from the anxiety increased a hundredfold by the desire not to desire so madly to go to Oran to the point of renouncing desiring to go to Oran, seen from the premonition that by dint of fearing desiring too madly going to Oran I would end up falling ill which would put a medical end to my torment – Algeria – and keep me in a hospital – France – the little lion that opens the door to our house in Oran is the size of a monster. The enlargement of the lion as effect of the return and its confinement in a dusty corner of the forgetting of Oran added to the inverse enormity that is to say not the emergence out of forgetting but the swallowing up of the lion that is to say of devouring Love in the entrails of the Python which the whole work of Proust predicts, this doubly unfortunate destiny, this double engulfing lies in wait for the foolhardy traveler who transgresses the surrounding wall of time. I am forewarned.

How to resist the love that lies in wait for me, how to avoid wanting to move forward between the teeth, lie down on the tongue let myself salivate dissipate ruminate on the lion's palate, in its palace in front of which I always found myself begging, first in Oran at the mouth of Rue Philippe, lion before, lion before the door, how not to surrender myself, how to surrender myself without surrendering either to being swallowed by Algeria or else to being swallowed by forgetting, I am forewarned, I have the choice between two swallowings. I am recommended, re-commanded by death.

When I was born in Algeria, I was deposited in front of Love into which I passionately desired to enter, I spent years in front of its chops between its paws, I was born outside in front of its teeth. I loved a lion like a dream, myself I was the shimmering and frail haze of the dream, the lion was the reality. My native fatal exalgeriance, if I must, is my originary withdrawal.

Everything was closed, I climbed in the cliffs, I threw myself against the Fromentin cliff, on the other side I saw Zohra, immobile, huddled, the lion is a bronze doorknocker, one strikes two strong knocks, one has in one's hand all the strange force of the irresistible call, its lowered head, the door opens, she enters, what I must do is: go out.

The more I think of Algeria, the more it grows, the more I see how small France is, the more Algeria stretches, crouching near the door-frame, grows larger each time I think of it the way a long-sleeping torment wakes up as a wild beast.

I understood that I was going toward *The Lion*. It was now just a matter of days. Ten days.

Zohra doesn't call, but what does it mean "to call"? Everything is overgrown, says my mother. Take pruning shears. Myself I am busy, it is my mode of being. I am proceeded by metaphor, I do battle with my bushes. The bushy undergrowth is my Algerian heritage. Neither blood right nor right of the soil – the right of the unconscious. Something of my undergrowth must come from my Algerian impossibilities. The undergrowth is what invades the mind when one can't be otherwise except on the side of the other side, one has no other side but the other side

She doesn't know what I owe her. I don't know what I owe her. She did exactly what my secret desire wished and that I would have wished to be able to desire if I could have disincarcerated myself from my algeriance. In 1957 I thought Zohra is in prison, what a relief, I thought I was dreaming, it was as if I was being in prison, in reality, finally, finally really being in being, whereas I have always been and I am with a prison stuck to me, I am in prison born, separated born from the prison earned, I was born deprived of prison, shut up outside the scene of the right to combat and to liberation-by-prison, what is Zohra going to say, I said to myself, if I find her address. I can't after all say to her, to see you in the first row in front to the left in the miraculous class, that was my spectral dream. I was thinking in an internal prison about the external prison. You can't imagine the weakness of the wishes of a specter, wishes are also powerless, they can only hope with a look. One cannot will for the other and yet my specter willed. How not to be on the side of the other.

When Zohra is in the Casbah in 1956 my mother the midwife is in the Casbah, my mother delivers the women in the Casbah, my specter is in the Casbah, with my mother on one side, Zohra is in her hiding place, I am not in the Casbah, I am my mother on one side on the other I am Zohra in the maze where death and life relay each other to give life. I don't know in which life I dream.

The Casbah goes up says my mother, I liked it, I crossed the donkeys that were taking down the garbage, the four-legged garbage men, I climbed up, my colleagues didn't go in the Casbah, the Algerian women, they were afraid of being attacked, I went out says my mother and I found an Arab on the ground dying because someone had just shot him, I opened my midwife's bag he was dead, a workman who was passing by.

In 2005 I get up every day into worldwide desolation. For a few moments solitude covers the whole earth, I miss the body. Then my mother returns. She is still there I say to myself, she is sleeping, but she is still going to wake up. I am going to hear the shuffling of her slippers in the kitchen climb up to me the way the crowing of the cock stops the shadows, the most comforting sound in the world, the midwife climbs up, pain is going to find a response, at that moment a door slams in the lower world, the shuffling begins, the first measures, my breathing rises, it's not today that I will be executed

Then awakens in the right-hand corner of the study the thought that salvation does not last long. The end of Maman awaits me. Soon the cock will have its throat slit. She is sitting across from me on the other side of the desk. I watch her watching *The Battle of Algiers*. She has headphones on for the sound. Her face: motionless, concentrated, unreadable. She says nothing. "I shouldn't have let myself get dragged in. I detest war films" my mother says.

I will not go to Algiers without my mother. It's too late. It's time, for the first time, I could and that is impossible.

Why does one call too late? Why does one decide to call too late? I call Toolate. I see its roar coming. My mother says: I detest war, all wars, and war films. She doesn't see Necessity. She has posted herself at the entrance of life. I observe the exit.

Why doesn't Roland pick up his telephone until after the amputation of the best part of himself?

At the beginning one doesn't hear anyone moaning, at the end one doesn't see anyone.

In 1956 I was euphoric and there was no one to whom I could tell the name of my euphoria. In 1954 I wept over all the first astonished dead those who say "why are you killing me?" In 1953 at the Madrague restaurant-café, I was on the side of the one who said to the one who was beside me: "why do you address me as *tu*?" I was beside myself. If I could have called my father, but he was too dead. My mother was in the Casbah, she was living in complete innocence like a nanny goat in the scrubland with young rabbits. If I had had a pistol at the Madrague

I sense today the secret taste of my joyous feeling from 1956, I had the taste of the just man by proxy, the taste of honey and saddened blood during that dream of not being in the middle of a dream in my bed.

Why isn't Roland altogether Olivier? Why does he wake up when he has changed color, he is wan, pallid, his very pale blood trickles the whole length of his body, he falls to the ground, amputated stabbed to death. When he has lost so much blood, from neither near nor far can he see clearly enough to be able to *recognize anyone whatsoever*. When he meets his friend he strikes him on the top of his helmet, on the precious stones and he splits it into two halves all the way down to the noseguard – but without reaching the skull.

My mother takes off the helmet of headphones. Why do you show me these wars? She leaves me. I look at these wars to split myself into two halves.

– Why doesn't anyone recognize anyone, do you do it on purpose? – Oh now I hear you speak, now too late, I have struck you. The world is full of our amputations.

Why didn't I send my letter to Zohra in prison? My letter remained locked up in my congenital prison. Why didn't Zohra telephone? We split ourselves into two halves, without reaching the skull

– Zohra has not telephoned? F. doesn't recognize the laws of the contretemps. – It is still not too late, I say.

Afraid of striking the top of the helmet, on the precious stones set in gold, afraid of striking my mother with Zohra and conversely afraid of doing it on purpose, one can't do otherwise, afraid of losing blood, the other blood

On one side I am on the side of Zohra the other, on the other side, my other side of the other side, I noted in a supreme effort to reunite myself with myself, I am to the side, born to the side, I noted, in the white notebook with bible paper that my beloved gave me the first day of before-Algiers. An all-white notebook for suffering. It does me good to write what hurts me on this paper soft as your skin.

Everything-that-will-nevermore-be-able-to be awaits me in Algiers, the realm of Maman. When Maman was wise-woman in the Casbah, Rue d'Isly, Rue Ben M'hidi Larbi, all those beings who were born, staggered, fell. The intense existence of what will no longer be able to be. One becomes a street. To run along Maman, her streets.

– I'm calling you late, says Zohra – Come, I say.

For the last ten days in Paris, every evening saying to oneself: I call H. it's always this present that fades away, this present that dreams and doesn't believe. "I call H." and at that moment, no call. Finally she will not have done it. Every evening she doesn't do it. Each evening a phantom. Phantomally there are ten phone calls at Z.'s house. Finally all of a sudden, the eleventh day, she does it. The number. Throw of the dice. Just before leaving. If I had not been there. If I had not answered. If I had answered distantly. She calls very late. She put all the chances for failure on her side.

93

I say: Come.

It is neither an order, nor an imperative, nor a present, nor a prayer nor an appeal. It is the first word that comes, that may come, that makes come what is going be the "we" that ever since the Lycée Fromentin could never be pronounced. The Lycée Fromentin was the name of the appearance of world, neither mine, nor hers, Fromentin the prefabricated world, a platform, a borrowing, the provisional-world set down over the abyss between worlds, caused by all those blind and blinding worlds that tottered on the same stage without touching each other, without reading each other, where the individual in transit detached from her or his origins, detached from the present where one sojourned, sought how to put an end to this present of appearance, this appearance of world, these cohabitants who could never have a sequel, who were already definitively passed into the appearance of being present in the *lycée* classroom. I can still smell the heavy scent of the recesses, the acridness of the animal silences, the beasts on the lookout, each one for herself beneath her smock, in those courtyards and walkways where the individual moved constantly heavily armed like a castle on a chaotic chessboard. One spoke on the diagonal, squared off, one thought only about being done with this story, with history, everyone with his or her history approaching the end, each person in this forgery all strapped up by force was approaching the last chapter. To get free of the class-as-mass at all costs, forever.

– Come, I say. – I'm coming, she says. Fifty years after the last chapter.

And right away afterwards, I note it down, she arrives early. I descend quickly, her small silhouette in profile before the glass door. Right away we embrace. It is the first time in our life and in our histories, we do not know whom we are embracing. We are finally for the first time ahead of what will come.

94

Victor Hugo notebook. *A classic suit. A small hidden emerald scarf. Hair: her hair. What was hidden beneath her hair. Details make destiny. Eyeglasses. She has trouble recognizing my face. I used to have another. The eyeglasses, that was me. Her slow voice. Her French: a perfect perfection: her paradoxical imperfection: lack of a lack. She will have chastised it.*

To cross a crevice fifty years across and several centuries deep some of them Occidental others Oriental, one must speak three hours precipitously without letting a tenth of a second's silence corrupt the weaving of one discourse in the other, for one must pass from one side to the other simultaneously at the same instant then cross back from the other side to the other side without posing oneself down, that is to say, without ever posing any questions to oneself, responding to each other, before any question, responding thus keeping up the rhythm of the narrations at a speed of life or death for one must go terribly quickly in order to adjust the pasts and fasten them lightly to each other so as to avoid the fatal hesitation, for this at the same time speak to and listen hear understand explain enlighten each other open oneself sweep away the mists, the vapors of ignorance and misunderstanding on each side at top speed guess the dangers, respond, get out in front of the trembling, make the truth for the other, make the other truth, at very great speed, the most difficult is to listen while still talking, to say I while thinking only you, to give oneself so as better to receive, all those maneuvers that one has never in one's life experienced and that must be executed with the brilliant mastery of trapeze artists, and this for three hours. But these three hours last ten minutes, it seems to us, that means that the speed of the crossing is multiplied by eighteen. In this first moment we describe those zappearances taken for real persons in the two camps. First of all we call them up, from there we deconstruct them, during this time we quickly and soberly paint self-portraits of what is essential. Everything that I cannot imagine, never could imagine, separated from imagining by an unimaginable ignorance. Once the first unveiling was accomplished, we have tea. The event rises very high above us. I cannot see the end of it.

All of a sudden I feel a sharp retrospective concern for Z. and H. these two beings banished as they were at Fromentin, these disguised ones feeding on rage, banished into two so dissimilar banishments, separated into two so different separated separations, enclosed in two enclosures of such different nature at the idea that they could have died before having finished telling each other their story. Today the separations are still alive, I say to myself, the enclosures still breathe their suffocating breaths on our lips, fear and anger still smolder beneath time, differently, similarly. But tomorrow, in fifty years, the gravity that makes us want to drink tea together will have become slight and negligible. It's like Rue Ben M'hidi Larbi, street of the Clinic d'Isly on the one hand, street of maternal Births and Deceptions, on the one hand, street of Fright, Regret, and Tragedy on the other. I go up the street on both sides. The metamorphosis of a being into a street is a question of months.

I was with you I say, but I was not with me. I was in a violent, severe, furious, trembling hope on the subject of you. Unbeknownst to me. I was the unsubject of Indignation

At last the letter to Zohra Drif has arrived, I say to myself, I no longer recall what I scribbled in 1957 or in 1960, nor what finally appeared, I know that it was always very improvised, not reread, spontaneous I don't recall if I thought that it would have an end. This thought of the end of a letter that I had imagined during fifty years, that had known me very young, then when I had changed griefs, styles, ruptures more than once more than one life, which didn't change, caused me to feel an anxious astonishment. It was as if I myself had received a totally improbable, posthumous letter, which told me to come on behalf of prehistoric Oran, making itself the different Echo of everything I was sure I had lived, and changed everything about what I had believed to be the long ago recorded meaning of my story. I was tasting the last rays of an incredulity.

Last walk "before-Algiers" with my mother in the park. I go
to get her. She hasn't waited for me. Early. Her small silhouette outside in front of the glass door, her face gay. I could be
happy I thought. Everything that stands between this "could"
and me: Algiers with absences. Without her. Without J.D.
Without. I note in the Toward Algiers Notebook, a notebook
with sails, giant sailboats on a skysea. I am in the half-dinghy
small as a fingernail cut off on the lower right of the cover.
The other half of the dinghy is not in the notebook. All
round the deserted park my mother keeps telling the story
of Madame B. a midwife in Algiers. Going down to the park
near the railroad she discovers that Mme B. is taking mor-
phine. Going back up she takes Mme B.'s place in the Casbah.
We are approaching the street-cleaning trucks that make an
ear-splitting noise. This doesn't prevent my mother from
continuing her inaudible narration. Between two trucks she
says you think I'm going to stop the story of Mme B. in the
Casbah which is making me hoarse? Well you're wrong. Mme
B.'s son had a charming wife as we turn round the lake he got
a divorce a bastard. The Milk Bar bomb that killed Mme B.'s
daughter-in-law. You didn't hear it. Of course I went to the
Milk Bar but not often. I wasn't that fond of ice cream. I'm
going to tell you: I didn't think anything. A woman is in labor.
It's midnight at Clos-Salembier. I get in my car. I meant
to tell you: excuse me that I repaired your chopping board
despite my ninety-six years. This way. She drags me, guides
me, has me visit her unknown neighborhood. One day there
was a demonstration suddenly gun shots. French troops who
had fired, there was a French doctor bent over a wounded

Arab, they shot at him and killed him in his white coat. I got out of there quick. Killing isn't a good way to defend yourself. The Algerians the way they treated women, bastards. In front of the supermarket I react badly there's a large funeral wreath in front of the glass door. You can't stand the truth says my mother. We go in. The worst bastards the guys in the OAS like the anti-Semites they boasted about the Arabs they killed even sixteen-year-old boys in the back. We don't buy anything. Man is like that, says my mother. We go out.

Where was I? When was I? Yesterday? Tomorrow? I could only approve of my mother while going from Rue d'Isly to Rue Ben M'hidi Larbi I could only approve of Zohra, I thought, when I am in one life she gives in the other, I react badly in front of funeral wreaths, when I spend the night in Algiers without being there, I always get up before dawn, before before, I do not spend the *night, I am it. I do not find my truth, someone tells me it is in the back of the room to the right, I cross the room, I see the landscape from afar, the sea raises its waves, it's sumptuous, the way the city raises its buildings like waves, I scan the vastness, my head turned toward the beauty behind the window, if only I could sit down, contemplate, but there is no room all is full, not a table, not a chair, where is my truth? it's probably that way says the café waiter, further on, to the right, I plunge into a dark corridor feeling my way, the moment I lean on the wall a shower is set off, I'm soaked, so that's how it is with my Algerrancy, for nights on end I am almost there, I start over, I am not discouraged by the hotelkeeper I circulate for a long time wet without ever finding my room again where I left my open suitcase bag papers books, eyeglasses, everyone shows patience and friendliness I will certainly end up by*

whereas in Oran I am in a plane. Oran is incredibly rich. We are flying on the ground passing in front of shops with lavish storefronts and what if I settled down in Oran? suddenly the plane oh! dives under a bridge, a very low tunnel, almost a tube. In Oran people fly fast, dangerously, skillfully, they don't back away from anything. Oran is strong. I admire it. If ever I get out of the plane I would like

among all the newspapers in Algeria read L'Echo d'Oran. *What touched me, the gothic characters of its title how can it be the echo of itself since time immemorial, echo of* L'Echo d'Oran, *and me the echo of the echo of the echo of Oran, therefore I am.*

I have never been so close   *Si jures*

I sit down on my suitcase. And what if I didn't arrive, what if I didn't land, what if I didn't reach, didn't touch didn't feel, Algeria? What if everything were dead? And perhaps only the dead alive?

This voyage is not a voyaging. Is a foraging.

In the next shot I see myself sitting on the ledge of the fountain without water, across from the exit at the Algiers airport. I am waiting. I am waiting for myself. Z. is waiting for me. But there is. There are: the birds. And: the palm trees. The cries of the swifts. It is too late, finally it is too late, it is my hour. A tall blind man in a white gandoura. The same one. What awaits me. I recognize him. These is always a tall elegant ageless blind man in a white gandoura. And the water noise of the Arab voices.

The camera is looking, I do not look at what it is looking at. What looks at me down to the bottom of my soul, to the point of bursting the membrane of the unconscious to the point of piercing my resistance in the back, to the point of moving back up through my blood to the point of knot-having-seen, all the way to the secret navel of my life, the point where it attaches itself to the Unknown, that thickest point in the fabric of dreams that will have made up my life, when I arrive there, so close to the end of my journey, I am

Algerian Jews (frenchified

so exhausted, I have shed so much of this blood retained for years, that I fall on my knees.

The camera doesn't see the abysses. I fall.

And the sound of the severed source. My father's two languages, severed. Arab, Hebrew. –ab. –brew. Arbrew. How does one mend a voice? I lend an ear. –near.

The crossing of my mother, I noted "But that night, furtively, I left, she didn't." _To be placed there where I leave so furtively that the departure is stolen from my mother, from the narrative, as if from myself, this confession made by Augustine running away from North Africa beyond his mother then by J.D. representing to himself his mother's tears the day after his furtive departure as if he were in the room weeping with her over this impossible separation. I will add that my mother, Ève Klein, unlike Jacques Derrida's mother who inherited after the cited mother the legacy of Ève, seeking while wailing what she has given birth to while wailing, will never have touched my ears with the overly carnal regrets of which Augustine complains. Which makes crossing the Mediterranean even more difficult to do on my side, and more paradoxical._

This mother in oneself that one must cross as my mother must have crossed her mother to reach Oran, without which there would be no prize, no bonus.

When just before the departing flight Z. asks me on the telephone for a list of places that I want to visit I don't hesitate for a second. As if she had asked me my name. As if I were answering the question who are you?

Who in me chose _naturally_ my Algiers names? The head, the trunk, the members, the sex, the heart, presented themselves before I thought.

101

Later, when I return to Paris, I will establish the list of the places that I would have sworn were vitally dear to me, and where I will never have been, to my surprise.

At the Algiers airport. I am sitting on the edge of the fountain without water, the swifts are whipping the air stretched between my two landscapes, *ashkoun ashkoun ashkoun*, time goes round the past is now French, I have left it. It is I who the swifts are calling.

I needed a letter to Z. that was a letter from Z.
A letter small enough to go to a large country
All the larger all the smaller
Well this letter is still on the run
It cries at the airport
Ashkoun ashkoun ashkoun ashkoun. who
Never heard a country cry so loud
So many birds, so many voices
France is so silent sitting
Sitting in the dining room dining
Everyone in their thoughts
Who? who? who? who? Is it
Who is it you, you, you, how fares your mother in you
Your brother in you, and the children in you, the country
how fares
Say say say say
Extinguished the birds of France sitting
At the church but there I don't go in.
I call Zohra. *Shkoun?* Who?
As soon as I arrived at the Algiers airport
The birds were given back to me
I had misplaced them in the silence
of France
As soon as the birds screamed

102

Who is it who are you who you are
I replied
It's I yes it's indeed I
All these months of me's without me
All these me's left
In my mother's keeping

But not one donkey.

It is a talking country I say to my brother

In principle in what follows of my Echo of Algeria I speak
of no landscape because it's a matter of passions not views. I do
not speak of the light and eloquent friends, metamorphoses of
birds into guides who truly carried me with their wings at an
incredible but necessary speed from one point to another of
the thallus every day. They are of the day. They drop me off
at the border of a chasm, at the edge of an eye, a page, let me
go alone all the way to the Unknown, wait for me with the car
at the portals of the night that I rummage through. Alone. I
recall them, we are in the call and the recall. But this book is
the work of forgetting.
Never have I encountered a book that opposed me with such
a dense, lively, rocky resistance, I use up a titan on every page. It
must be, I say, that I presented myself before the Forbidden.

The military Tribunal says Zohra, the disciplinary council
of the Lycée

It awaits me since I have returned from Algeria,
interminably

I approach by way of daily wanderings, by dilapidations of hours spent digging beneath the paper to find again my point of departure, I keep my eyes on the square opening carved in the depths, where stands the Head, every day I hope the day after I will be fit to go to the heart of this trance.

I wonder who, except J.D., could have imagined, could imagine everything that managed to happen, I will note when one day I am back in Paris, such as eddies, mutations, seisms, reshufflings, turn-arounds once and for all, during those eight days spent in Algeria. I knew that I had lived only seven days, I will note but I always said eight, as if that had some hidden importance, eight, or seven, or so as to say more than seven as if what were improbable in seven days became probable on the eighth

When I was there I felt surrounded by light touches, invisible thefts of books, bats, the dead who never leave me, millions of Algerians past mixed with the smiling passers-by in the Rue Ben M'hidi Larbi, in the Rue d'Arzew, it is especially human beings who upon contact with me and as I passed by all of a sudden took on eternity, coming and going with me in the air of that Algerian time which stretches without interruption its millennia washed in the very salty water of our sea, to the point that, when she opens for me the door of her apartment at 54 Rue Philippe, I find Mme Benaouf resembles Monica the mother of Augustine and I am enchanted: the same restrained vivaciousness, the same warm timidity that makes appear even younger the face on which no wickedness has ever carved a wrinkle, I find again the milky whiteness of the skin whose familiar luminosity the son must have contemplated so often each evening before falling asleep. Mohamed: the son. I noted.

Such a journey either it's India or it's Palestine. Apocalyptic in advance. When one is there, one is not there: that's the apocalypse. One is not/present/in the present. One is in Super. In superpresent, in supervision, in superspeed, in supersense, in laceration. When I am sitting on the metal chair, at the Fishermen's restaurant, La Pêcherie of Oran (across the street Gas Station) where there is and even though there is the "problem," that is to say a sewer, which comes back no matter how repressed it may be, even though the sewer brings back with it the precious retinue of problems-sewers that decorated my streets when I lived in Algeria, even though I am partaking with Belkacem Chafi and Sid Ahmed, the family attributed to me by a decree of the apocalypse, six large red mullets, a ton of shrimp, as much calamari, I noted thinking of my mother, even though the spigot in the back of the room washes my hands, an aspect of hospitality that took up its place in my heart as immediately as the jam pot that once it begins to move in the night of the Proustian narrator is going to take its place on the shelf of the dream, the chair is the same chair on which my uncle sat sixty years ago, the "problem" hasn't changed, I am not the same, I am not sitting on the chair, I am levitating slightly without being able to do anything about it, I have *not yet* arrived on this chair I am fluttering over it, I am trying to prevent this levitation from being detected, I stand up, I crouch between the tables, I adopt a gentle one-eyed cat, I cut up a mullet in front of the eternal gentle one-eyed cat who follows me wherever I sit down in the world, that isn't done my families will think, but Belkacem et Sid Ahmed will not say so, only my mother will express her reprobation, and I don't disapprove of her. I am linked, intimately, passionately, to the blind and the one-eyed, this fate has been decided for me, at my birth in Oran, will I ever know why?

I noted.

I was not "present" in the present. I was on loan. One does not become present except in the past, I noted, now that I was

105

present after.

I was so pressed in the present that I didn't have time to be there

I will venture out. It was my country, but I was their stranger. I entered vestibules, I went toward the ladies who command these places, strong and furtive persons, I presented myself as a visitor, I was received kindly and with curiosity by the children, I was led toward obscure regions, in the back, I felt the warm and mysterious spirit of the welcome, I dove into the depths, I followed my young years feeling my way, I walked a long time, far from myself, burning with curiosity. I saw schools of children as surprised and curious as I. I spoke French. They were gay, interested as I had been, yesterday. I knew that at the end of the street I would have to wake up, go out, return to the other side, in the other country. I was already losing my country . . .

How many journeys there are in the journey
We are coming close. I am guiding the chauffeur who is guiding me. Wahib, I say. He exists in reality. Thin in reality. I go pointlessly to Clos-Salembier. It is not there. That is not where I want to go. Clos-Salembier doesn't exist. I don't believe in Clos-Salembier. Already in 1948 I didn't believe in Clos-Salembier in reality. My father having carried off the Clos-Salembier world with his death. When I went to Clos-Salembier nevertheless in 1954, then in 1964, then the other times, it was not there. I went to the top of the hill, I started down the Ravine of the Wild Woman, I turned into the streets of flowers without flowers, I said "has someone been here? Has there been Doctor Cixous?", of course no echo. No flowers no regrets. An obedience. I stopped ever wanting to go there in 1970 the last time. I have already written this in another book. What is a voluntary lapsus? To go in spite of myself to Clos-

Salembier to see the house that had no longer existed for quite some time, whose total disappearance and replacement by a tall building without opening I discovered in 1970, thus to go see *About* the annihilation of all remaining trace not a one anywhere in *Schmidt* spite of myself I can't prevent myself from doing it. It's not me, it's my body. I am my body, I follow my body. Yes says my body let's turn to the left, my body is one body with the boulevard, I don't recognize anything, my body murmurs to him Télemly, yes, this round-about, let's take it, the tracing once awakened my body has the memory I have the forgetting, a memory in the abdomen in the neck in the hips leads, feels without seeing for everything is now overbuilt. The one who is leading is this primitive body, the being of contact, the one who takes command after curfew, who climbs mountains before which I stand paralyzed, who has an immemorial pact with the lines of the earth, who swims to distant cities as if it were led into the unknown by the secret paths of generations, it senses that we are going to arrive in front of the Cemetery, and we pass by a closed site that bears the title "Christian Cemetery." We are coming close. In the end, there will be no end. Were it up to me personally I would say to Wahib let's stop, beyond the Cemetery begins what is no longer, but in reality the body continues. It has an agreement with the emaciated body of Wahib, the superhuman stubbornness of beings who are worn down to the bone. Look out! vibrates, my body, quick, turn, follow the track, to the right go, it can only be here, right away. Stop! Here? There. That was. That can only have been. Wahib gets out, limps. Limps for me. Without falling asleep one has sunk one thinks one is awake. Didn't see Wahib get out, I was sleeping. A thousandth of a second, to make the past pass. Wahib on the sidewalk. Not me. Nor my body. It's here? My head turns toward where it is not. 54 D says the corner of a little building. 54 is the fate of Cixous. Everywhere we have lived, it was 54. A shop. Wahib is talking. I want to stop him but I'm sleeping.

*How do all these deconstructionists live such
a serindi...dous / fortuitous lives*

Can't open my mouth. I want to say "that is not done, to act the ghost, no, to enter the home of the living, to disturb to say I used to be I had I was, no, let's take off" I want to return appropriately to inexistence, but I am not awake, at least not here, not 54 D, the dream is accomplishing everything I do not wish. It is the dream of Wahib, Z.'s chauffeur on the one hand, on the other the emissary of the emaciated people to whom my father belonged. The shopkeeper, an upholsterer, he is outside, not his store, for it's a dream shop, in his fifties, a rotund white soft-spoken man sporting a spotted red T-shirt, an unexpected visit, roused from his bed for no client does he expect, warm, a round little talkative sun. Wahib somber thin elegant. Cixous says the one Cixous says the other. Cixous? I say to myself. Cixous! exclaims Monsieur Aïssa. My body takes a step. Oh Monsieur Aïssa tells the rapt audience. Wahib and me. There was a large garden here immense flowers spilled over the hedges fruits dove from one tree to the next there were so many of them lemons in the mimosas your feet were in violets the rich soil took pleasure beneath people's gazes. Medlars. Cixous! 10,000 square meters! exclaims Monsieur Aïssa. I too feel the enthusiasm. The author of this garden that is to say of this story that is to say of this dream garden is Monsieur Aïssa's grandfather. 10,000 square meters I murmured. I am afraid of waking my co-dreamer. 10,000 square meters? Monsieur Aïssa says, weakening. Now cut into two. He has 600 square meters. We count softly. All the same I say, you would have thought 10,000 when you saw the flowers, and we granted ourselves also a dromedary since there were date palms. And all these marvels are now the inheritance of Monsieur Aïssa since I am his witness. The flowers the fruits the animals this whole vast paradise slumbers in the rolls of fabric of Aïssa and son. Yes. Monsieur Aïssa is a magnificent heir. I see the dream. The sumptuous visiting card, the moderate shop, the prodigious sign, Upholstery by Tayeb and Aïssa, arabesques.

Made to Order, Repair And Decoration
of all Living Rooms Armchairs, Chairs
and Benches Blinds, Carpets
and Padding Installation of all Net Curtains
Manufacture of Living Rooms
Moroccan and oriental

For proof of the All a delicate vignette surrounded in heavy gold opens on the curtains a stroke of genius of the stage director, promise. Garden of Eden, continuation.

A modest happiness takes hold of me. My dream has a lot of imagination. I didn't expect such a faithful metamorphosis. "Installation of all" transports me. Net curtains, that is, *Voilage!* Some god has passed this way. Come! Come in! I say no, I say yes. One mustn't ask more than perfection. I am surely going to fall. No. But I say Yes to red Monsieur Aïssa enchanted enchanter. I follow him in the staircase, I go further, I go further. Detritus. Stretched out on the stairs. Detritus sleeping. Are at home but in the stairwell, like dogs. As always in my dreams. One acts as if one didn't see and perhaps one doesn't see. In the end, one often arrives outside: interior terrace, veiled by walls. To the right the horizon. In the distance somber green moist densely grown the woods of the Wild Woman. Recompense. I had never seen that, Monsieur Aïssa. When one is right on the ground below in the first materials of creation, one doesn't see the sex of the gods. I call my brother, he doesn't answer, hello here is our childhood, he doesn't answer. I call my mother. Where? At Clos-Salembier. I have just struck a blow at my mother. I say the violent, impossible, frightening thing to her: it's alive. We lived on death, we went on without turning round, we went away from the salt and the rock and we came to Paris. And I say to her: the earth moist with my father's sperm, has stayed moist so long after his death, I see minuscule slender hands with long white fingers coming up, they signal to me by waving all the thin and living

109

fingers of sperm: that the Sperm survives. The earth that was killed first of all beneath the heavy, closed building, what I saw in 1970, has raised itself up. The citadel has been chased away. Residences, shops, inhabitants buzz around 54 D. I strike my mother with stupor and I can't take her in my arms. I pass her Monsieur Aïssa as if in a dream, they are face to face. Good day Madame Cixous, good day it's kind of you, the unparalleled ability of my mother: to adapt herself to the devastating event in less than two seconds. She takes what comes in stride. We are sitting on the terrace's square bench. A rooster cries out. I say: can you hear the rooster? Yes says my mother. I say: he is still there. My mother says: the same rooster? – Blessed be he I say a sixty-year-old rooster. The white rooster cries out. I don't see him. Is he white? I say. Yes says Monsieur Aïssa. So I'm dreaming. So I'm not dreaming: it's indeed a dream that is happening in reality. If the dog barks, I will say nothing, I will hide my tears. A dog barks. I get up. I am standing on the terrace built on the earth where sleeps lost here or there overlooked Fips my dog who died for humanity. I hide my tears. Standing on the terrace with nose raised panting moist toward the sky that never answered, I salute Fips vaguely, in case he was running around the clouds with the speed of a deer. Come back, says Monsieur Aïssa. Will I come back? I say no. No says Yes.

It's like forgetting. Not forgetting. One cannot give oneself the order. One must move heavy furniture, get down to the earth where we sleep perhaps believing that we are awake perhaps believing that we are asleep, dig delicately into the humus until one finds perhaps the little handful of Sperm that has not yielded to death. It's not impossible that one can succeed – only every forty years perhaps. It's long, coming back.

The pain of leaving Fips alone in the without garden, when will it be extinguished?

Tell Monsieur Aïssa, there is someone, there below, beneath the shop who was Fips my father's son, I am sure he will understand. So I will begin thinking of Monsieur Aïssa, suffering at the idea that we all die, we are abandoned, we remain alone, Monsieur Aïssa as well in forty years, will there be someone there?

From there to the Lycée Fromentin with Zohra
Right after that to the Lycée Bugeaud now reconquered as Abdelkader
– But with Zohra that's not where I want to go most urgently
Where I can go only with no one, where I can go only later, without strength and without address –
Right after that to El Biar
From there to the Jardin d'Essai
As if I couldn't go most urgently where I want to go or die
All the attempts noted in the Voilage Notebook. What a voylage we are on.

We hear the rooster. My mother laughs. She hears herself laugh. She laughs her laugh, very loud. Louder and louder. It's the rooster she laughs. How funny it all is. The past. It's funny.

I didn't see the rooster. But the camera saw him. It's funny. This camera that sees what I don't see. I'm dreaming. It pecks away. It stretches its neck. I cut. Off.

When I return to Paris, I will see myself seeing the rooster with my mother, all of sudden, with my mother I will see myself at Clos-Salembier, in the staircase, I will see myself not seeing the rooster from the top of the staircase in the film, to the right, above my head, the head of the white rooster, behind which one will make out the Ravine of the Wild Woman, then I will see the whole rooster that I did not see, on the screen, the rooster and me, in the same shot, I will see that I do not see.

111

– The rooster! It's where the garden was! It's crazy! It's unbelievable! My mother is doubled over laughing in Paris

I no longer know what time it is.

– Have you eaten any fish at the Admiralty fishery? They have fresh red mullet, says my mother, from this morning.

Tipaza? I can't do it. Too rich, too sumptuous, too pink, too blue the beauty too great, too present. The camera heads straight to the tiers. I sat down on a rock. Not to go all the way to the end. To let the camera have its treat. The good majesty will begin to take shape slowly the next day in the Voilage Notebook, the immense city summed up, lentisks, absinthes, it's through words that I will enter tomorrow, asphodels. At present I sing the cats under the tables while crouching under the tables of the restaurant in Tipaza.

I sing the cats, under the tables of the restaurant in Tipaza, where Monsieur Saïd is in despair about men who are becoming wolves for men from one day to the next, so thin small reduced wild, a hunger that leaps small faces with large ears in white and black, I cut up little pieces of liver, they throw themselves on the food under the tables weave under the tables on the rocks flee the brutal shoes purposely not seeing the cats fly on the roofs lighter than cats, I throw myself on the cats, country of birds country of cats, a slender, meager race seeking frenetically something to eat

Country of fish for my mother.

And the fourth day "what do you think of the Algerians?" this is my brother's question, my brother who is not in Algeria who is on the telephone. I didn't want to answer. I don't want to answer that question, I say. Why?

Pose de tout, installation of all, I repose my brother's question sent from my brother over there, here over there. Comes an answer: I don't think. About Algerians I don't think. About the French I think this and that, about the French French. About the Algerians I am here today, I am here, I don't think, what would I say about myself? About myself I think nothing therefore I am. Something in me is embraced, embraces. I have: the habit. Came back like the swimmer's movements in the sea, my native habit among the Algerians, like when in the water one bumps into the water, into the other, one laughs, my habit of being with them in the other

During the question I was looking the white lights shining on the black bay. I think: Algeria, life, death, shudder. Slimness, I say, youremember? – What, sister? says my brother. I say: Papa's slimness, their slimness, slimmed down from within, from within the nervous flame of the nervous soul, nervous people of the depths men champing at the bit of the soul youremember? There is also hunger, says my brother, malnutrition. On the other side, once on the other side one slackens a little and gains weight. It's men who hew themselves, the women nourish are nourished, sweetened with children.

I don't think about Algerians. I laughed. Or wept, it's the same thing. My whole life, it makes me laugh, Algeria. Or weep. Higher than the ground. The country boils. Overflows. An overflowing. Too much. Too many tears for the heart. The director of the theater of Oran owns the world, isn't that what it is when one has a sphere where all the visions of humanity are nestled, even though he takes refuge in the concierge's lodge, even though the crystal chandelier as big as an oak with crystal leaves hung by its root like the sun over the earth has been kidnapped, cut up into slivers of glass and resold in ten thousand pieces, the director of dreams in Oran weeps a large gush of tears. It is love he says. Simply the loved one, love.

Ask me rather what do I weep of the Algerians. Love. I would like to understand says my brother. The histories of Algeria says my brother, oof. When I tell my brother about

54 Rue Philippe, at the moment I embrace Linda Benaouf in the dining room where at the same time I see the star on the mosaic floor youremember, he has tears in his eyes. He would like to understand. The six black branches of the stars on which we spread our childhood, later copied onto red tissue paper then little by little raised from the floor to the sky of the magic lantern. There is also a goldfinch. So the house has indeed transmitted the signposts: here: the goldfinch cage. Our first death and our first death of love. Be careful of goldfinches because they are beings that the death of love kills. When Augustine was little he also wept over the very shimmering smallness of the body of the goldfinch from which the life had just flown. In his hand the warm, delicate being struck motionless by the last dream like the caressing and silent touch of the farewell. That's how things began weeping in this country, one feels death coming too early in this country

It is five in the morning. I am betraying myself. I am going to my native city. There has been no other possibility. The evening before the departure, before the return, before going, the very morning, I changed my mind. Airport. State: nothing. Who knows what will happen. Oran is so far away will I manage to bring it back today? I hope not. Thus I will not arrive by the train station. The train station of Oran: saved. Intact fabulous with grandmama all in black except for the shoe buckles, the horse-drawn carriage, the sooty hands. Airport. Every two minutes the loudspeaker announces the judgment: immediate boarding. One believes it. But there is no plane. One raises the body, immediate boarding, one puts it back down. One begins to think: what is the immediate? Clenched heart. Thus it is Oran and not Algiers that awaits me, that I await. One enters by twists into the propeller plane. Immediate takeoff. Stop! A mortal terror strikes me on the head: your watch! The fear of having forgotten your watch at the Saint-Georges Hotel, the certainty, the pain, of having for the first time ever taken the risk made the decision done the mad thing of bringing your remainder with me, of having brought it to see you with me, its docile face eternally immobilized, the violence of having secretly exhumed your watch from my drawer, of having plotted in secret with myself this transport of the sacred remainder, of having led it around, submissive, in the pocket now of some trousers, now of a blouse in which finally I forgot it, I left the face stopped at the end of time wrapped up in the blouse, and sitting buckled up in the prop plane, immobilized, I see it changed into a white talith with blue stripes, I see the cleaning lady enter room 313, the little embalmed, impotent body, a sole idea: arrive at the blouse where the adored remainder reposes, and not in Oran. In the plane I pray and do not answer. Orange juice? Anguish. Always, in place of living, this fear of losing again what remains to be lost.˙As if you were all that and all those I have to lose, this face made slightly swarthy by time, this silence, this body of striped cotton with imponderable arms. But on arrival, on the moving walkway of the little airport, you are there, in the suitcase and thus Oran. My hourless time.

Not only had I never imagined, I could never have imagined, not once in fifty years did I have the unacceptable thus invisible idea that I could see myself in Algeria without my mother because I would never have accepted it, but I had never had the idea that it might happen to me to wander in Al- without J.D. As for the idea of being in Al- without my brother, it was not unacceptable since it had never been envisioned, it would have been impossible for me to turn one way or another toward the Algeria with an inconceivable without-my-brother, I have never touched, inhaled, sought, suffered Algeria without his being half me, inhaling seeking suffering the same smells, the thirsts and their lemonades, perched in the same hermaphrodite medlar tree held together by a graft to which we have always submitted. And it is this supremely absurd hypothesis, this anomaly of the chromosomes of fate that is being realized. All the impossibles accompany me, and for lack of a brother at my hip I limp in Rue Ben M'hidi Larbi, I proceed into the throat of 54 Rue Philippe without the green eyes of my brother for the thick blackness as if at the next step, brutally falling I was going to wake up flayed from the melancholy that unjustly condemns me to injustice. In the proud and marvelous arteries of Algiers I trot along bent over with the tedious pack of the unacceptable on my back, the only donkey in the city is me. You can't imagine how heavy are the bodies of the phantoms that I carry burro-like. I pass by divided, loss is my rhythm, I open a wound in this country through which I send sentences toward absent ones I detour the blood of the present, right is with me but the just is in the other world.

And the beggars? Where? All of a sudden, I go down, I pass by the Main Post Office, I go back up Rue Didouche-Mourad, I look for the beggars, the blind, the amputated, the starving old women whose murmurs are more powerful than knife blades, where are those people who in the past held me frightened over the abyss, have you seen them? The donkey neither?

If I go to Oran where I don't want to go minus a brother it's because of the donkey who used to prophesy, from Rue Philippe to the Place d'Armes called in the past the Military Circle all the way to Rue d'Arzew, all the way to the Michelet market, that even dying from pain one bears witness all the same to the inhumanity that makes humanity, surely these fragile and necessary species survive in my native city I would like to believe, I believe in donkeyness.

"The fifth day I had the feeling that this journey had reached the end. I could have taken a plane for Paris without regret I didn't dare I was afraid of not having been to Oran and that that would become reproach shame and incomprehension among me. To be sure what I wanted to see, that which I wanted to see urgently on any condition, that, I had seen it in Algiers, the Life-Thing, I had seen it finally. I was afraid of never coming back but I didn't say it to myself. On the other hand if I went nevertheless to Oran, it would be easier for me in the future never to come back."

I noted this in the future past of the narrative that I would devise if later there came to be the book whose warm breath I felt approach my lips in the room of the Saint-Georges Hotel, it was four o'clock the birds would soon be waking up, finally people were quieting down a little, the camera was sleeping, I was with the notebook, alone with you, with you, with my absent ones, between Algiers and Oran as between you and me, I was undergoing for the seventh time the ordeal of the threshold that has not left me since I hesitated to my mother: *I will perhaps go to Algiers.* Now I noted, *maybe I will go to Oran.* I may be only as maybe, baby that I am, more maybe with each temptation. In the darkness I go down the hand-some, silent staircase. Am I dreaming? Am I awake? It's your theme no longer knowing on which bank you are, on which life, where life is?

I saw it come in. The book was sitting in the Moorish room. It stood up. I thought I'm dreaming, I see the book, it is going to dissipate when it gets close to me. I was content. It lingered. You are not dissipating? You are going to stay? Yes. Good, how not to believe it? But how to believe it? I circled around belief. Blessed be the unbelievable that comes to pass. I will not ask any question. You accompany me toward the exit of e great hall. Your dark well-chosen suit, in a second, I rec-ognized it, on the marble floor your silhouette, here people have a taste for dressing well. Outside the famous botanical garden. It's here that I noted the moods that my first book caused in me, forty years ago. The same bench. But you are not the same. I sit down beside the one who I was forty years ago, sitting bewitched by the griefs to come, in flight deep within her reverie, tasting the first notes of clandestinity. One hides in order to write. Within the curtains of wisteria con-cealing the one that I was going to be. I was crowned then by daturas with calices of seduction, one could begin to die from the intoxication of being born from a country where I knew I would never know the exact text of my role. But you are not the same. Forty years ago I was fleeing you a little, fearing you or else I feared not inventing you truly enough, not believing in you powerfully enough for you to be. I cast a glance, there is no one except the eucalyptuses and the magnolias so I dare, if you exist, because you exist, I sign, I kiss your mouth, my tongue on your mouth. We back away down the path. This time we kiss passionately this time your tongue in my mouth nothing resembles a resurrection so much as the passion of a book, and likewise the embrace of a book is comparable to a resurrection, why not say it? we are body to body, we are mad with passion, that's how it is the book, your tongue in my mouth, two me's, two months. I say to you are you going to stay in my mouth? Yes. You say yes in my mouth. It is not just an apparition, even if right afterwards the cunning forces of the dream carry me away, even if to escape an endless misfortune I am obliged to wake up. I write you close by. Don't forget the kisses were real, I noted. What moved me: your Arab air, dark, the dark fire, the well-groomed dark suit, your man-from-Algiers stylishness.

While I dream, the camera sleeps. What it doesn't see: it didn't see me running on borrowed time in the Jardin d'Essai. It didn't see me embrace you, wipe the dust from your face with my tears. It didn't see me refuse to climb the non-staircase at 54 Rue Philippe. What I give it to see: two hundred states of yellow pink red twilight the wedding ceremony of the sky and the sea celebrated from four o'clock to six o'clock at my window. This opera is not in guidebooks, it's not in the museums, it takes place only before the creation of humankind, when painting has not yet begun to translate the untranslatable. Perhaps it has drowned itself in the mystical blaze, where even the sun is eclipsed. I give it the araucaria, like a giant non-cross posted in front of the voluptuous bay, so large that the boats look like little jokes on the water. What I give the camera to see: the trunks of the ficus trees corseted with whitewash. Their cherished heads: always the same cut of the foliage and no one knows who has created the cut, the divine hairdresser, eternal style.

What I give it to see: not-me.

– I am frustrated, one never sees the sea says my brother, not one wave.

What I give to see: not-one-wave, the color of the impressions of eternal proximity, the sea on fire in golds, the silks in a dozen different pinks of the distances whose thickness will never be reduced. Sights from my Saint-Georges window. Renoir came to Algeria and he saw very well: the Ravine of the Wild Woman, portrait of the secret painted.

I paint the secret. A luxury of secrets. The luxuriance of secrets gathered into the volume of Algiers. I paint the journey in the journey.

No one has ever seen such a talking country and everywhere fountains of silence. Everyone talks so much here that one seeks the sudden freshness of the hour of nocturnal morning when speech is cut off. What the camera cannot see. When the immense bowl of passions overflows and finally drowns its fire.

I have not spoken of the Battle of Zohra, not spoken of the Battle of Algiers, not asked Zohra has not told me about this Battle, tells me about the Battle of Fromentin, me too the first battle, the first courtroom. The Battle of Ronceveaux on the other hand, the revenge of the Battle of Ronceveaux, our battle, for hours we pursue it, in the car on board which we are not, we don't see the First Empire Marshalls boulevards, we roll along like stones in the passes of the Pyrenees, we tumble down the gorge, leaning on the mountain Zohra weeps for Roland leaning on the mountain weeping for his fiancée and later weeping for his tears, like me I wept for my tears, which were not Christian. Zohra and Hélène, we were with the Preux, the Valiant Knight, but he was not with us. But Zohra keeps the word *preux* all the same. The handsome, motionless, masculine face, effigy of the useful being, in the pocket of her smock. Daughters of fathers

What brought us close was what separated us the war the same each one on her side I thought this while we were going down the narrow passages of the Casbah of which she was so proud, where she had not set foot in ten years, the handsome faces of the doors have changed into rust, says Zohra,

This body of the Casbah
Like a naked old woman
I am unhappy says Zohra
Like a hidden young woman
Seeing her die I am unhappy
This body of the Casbah
Furrowed
Three eternal young children at the fountain
Under the smashed letter-box.
The last letter killed it, which fired

Shell in the skull of the letter-box.
A tongue used to live in this skull
One can see the letter-box of Hamlet
Has crash-landed in Thebes Street
Direct flight Elsinore cemetery-Casbah
The box remains. No one would have wanted to do away
also with the nest
Neither living nor dead, silenced
Become nest
For ghosts
You cannot believe
How beautiful it was
Imagine marble slate
Jasmine
That are no longer anywhere
The body of the Casbah
Its elegant woman's body
Slender quick
Today out of breath
One cannot imagine it
Imagine
My amazement says Zohra
The first time
Between the different areas
Such airtightness
Imagine the battle
Between the houses
massacred
No one can imagine such a permeability
Between imaginations
Imagine what no one will ever see again
In the Casbah
Where I have not gone
In ten years

I don't want to die says Zohra
Without having seen it rescued
What can no longer be imagined
One can see it written on the gentle face of Monsieur
Hakim
The curator
When he gently caresses the model
Of the one who was
The One Who Was.
The slenderness of the limbs, the proud neck, Kasba
Chanted: Monsieur Hakim
Conducts minutely tender
Syllable by syllable the reconstitution
May he go on resuscitating her for a long time
I am unhappy she says
Everyone desired her, in turn,
Torn apart, burned,
Dynamited, pillaged,
All the way to the poem,
I am happy
I had not gone, says Zohra
To suffer, in ten years.
The skull remains beautiful
The tongue follows us while whispering
To the bottom of the stairs.
The eternal message that is careful never to address its
unknown addressee
"If God wills"

I hope you will come back, they say, if God wills, I hope that
you will that god will what you will, what he wills, what does
God will we don't know, God wills if, god wills something other
than god, all that we want is to want something other all the
same, here the Djezirs want terribly strongly, as if God didn't

want quickly enough or humanly what they want or too quickly, if God wills says J.D., if God wills, may He exist, I hope that He will decide to exist, to hope, that's the nickname of god, God if he decides will have to get used to the idea of the compromise.

To Ruth Beckermann I say:
I didn't use your camera
It followed me, it picked up scents, it was
Drawn to cracks, the secrets of the sidewalks
You will see in its story only us
Four-footed beings, propelled as we are
By the irreducible hope, of a salvation,
We rolled in the dust
We turned round
In the narrow vertical ramps
While rubbing against the walls
That you will see: the faults, the tilework that floats
You will see the following cats:
the patrol of six cats that stood in line
At the Michelet market in Oran
While waiting for their turn at the carcass
Of the fish gnawed on by the eldest
Besides the cats and the fish there was not
A lot to eat for free at the market
The stalls are slimmed down as in a dream
The seven cats of Tipaza already named
The shy cats of the La Pêcherie more fearful
Than the beggars
For there are beggars in Oran as I suspected
And in the hierarchy of Misery the cats catch on to the fact
that they are inferior to the lowest
Happy was the cat at 54 Rue Philippe,
Happy was the pasha mixed up with the fish nets
Piled on the dock of the Admiralty all red

And sleeping together
Only cat of the trawlers that go out after sardines
According to organized shortages.
In the end you will not see Adieu, the little grey cat
Come from Nowhere,
For how could he have crossed
That large desert gullied with motorways
In the knot of which the absurd hotel in Oran
Raises up its concrete confection, to come all alone
Tiny to present himself meowing at the forbidden
threshold
So as to signal to me the death in the soul.
When I tried to hold him for a moment with your camera
All that remained in front of us was his invisible appeal
Meowed, meowed, I look for him everywhere in vain
This your camera doesn't see, there is moreover Nowhere
To look for him because as soon as I go out the door it's
the motorway
You will have no image of Adieu, the spirit of the country.
I said to your camera, go, follow your inclination
I let it lift its nose, pick up the wind
Receive messages from below

And in Santa Cruz very close to the sky, but one is not
allowed to put one's feet on its feet protected by barbed wire,
in Santa Cruz, translation of the revered SantaCrousse of my
childhood, the height of heights never reached always aspired
to, your camera said no, it's too much I will not descend from
the most beautiful height possible, glory of the most noble
mountain in the world, I will not descend into the crypt, I want
to drink here, I don't remember the Spaniards or the faith or
the cross, the mass, does that interest me? no, the military
guards invited us the camera and me to enter the church, they
urged us to taste the mass, in their passion for hospitality, the

124

guards, since there was a mass it was for us, I prefer to stay with the four of you I said, and your camera followed, the two handsome, emaciated and tender-hearted soldiers and their two adored dogs we stayed side by side, the camera and me, Bicha, her male, and their two brotherly relatives, the six of us inhaling the air of the scrubland. The skinny yellow dogs who had their fill of the brush that's what I have to tell you about SantaCrousse. Until there arrived "the king," who is the king of the dogs and thus of the soldiers. "Here's the King" my military brothers murmured, so arrived a king, coming from the bottom of the mountain, as if springing up from the thick middle of the sea, as if crawling among the lentisks and terebinths, the calm and steady king who was a dog, reigning, unquestionably. And the king is called Jacques say the soldiers, that's how it is. You will see us side by side adoring embracing with a wide glance the city of Oran spread in a painting of giant blond stretches, like seven gods in love with the nymphs who used to perch in the old days on the tops of the maritime pines – they were the size of squirrels – to feast their eyes on the span of their dense beauties. Such a vast splendor, only kings and gods can be intoxicated by it, it's too beautiful for me said your camera, how can I paint what surpasses me, not even the Oranais can tolerate the immensity of their immensity. It is rare that the adorable Oran without pride goes up there to look at itself from the point of view of jealousy. Oran is good for being born I say to the tenderly animal men, Algiers is good for dying, I say. Algiers is not the same, they agree and all their eyes are wide and moist like my father's eyes. Enough. *Off.*

One doesn't see Zohra, says Ruth. From the point of view of the camera. But according to me this book sees only her.

I will let the camera say what it saw according to its own glance.

Did it think about the filth?

To my brother Pierre I say: I will tell you about the filth. I want to share the filth with you. Youremember Papa's "sentinels" that slumbered in the Baïnem woods? And what did they keep watch over, all the same not very zealously those stools placed along roadsides, a treat for the flies? Over what do they continue to keep watch? I am going to tell you. This is not what I came looking for. But I found them again and recognized them, where they had taken refuge, all the varieties of filth. Above the poem, at the bottom of the poem on the hillsides, in the stairways of Clos-Salembier, along the lace grillwork that encloses the Lycée Fromentin, along the wooded incline that descends from the waist of the building to the feet of the city in necklaces and bracelets of peelings to the neck of the beaches, offered, like truths that must not be spoken, like the words of warning of the prophets, reminders, powerful and powerless sermons to the prideful civilizations, that we all die two deaths, one awaits us on the last day, the other before the last day, we will have given ourselves the other death through corruption, sloth, and cowardice. How to speak of the manifest filth with the respect that is due to speech, and to warnings, when one comes from a country where filth is interior? Our filth speaks, idiomatically. All of us have Horror. Some of us throw it outside, others simmer it inside. All of us secrete evil and bad thoughts. Who can decide if it is better, for whom, where, to bury, at what depth, or drown, where, classify, forget, put away, hide, in what parenthesis, the undesirable proofs of our mortalities? How to judge the filth of others, is my tongue proper for translating properly the other properness? Youremember, I say to myself, 1955, year of repulsion, the difficulty of living among the Parisian lepers, of breathing the moisture the mildew and the fake rocks in the simulated parks, a blackened city I shivered that covers with rugs its worm-eaten floors, abundantly nauseating, but I had not yet met Montaigne nor learned reciprocity from my cat myself I was lepered, I was outside, I was outfilthed in excision between the far side and the near side of the pyrenees, I remember I say to myself 1955, the year of from worse to worse

To my brother I say what separates these two countries that are not mine, not yours, that make the day, that make the night, that make love, and its opposite, in our interior cities, is nothing, it's a cup of water, multiplied by the streams of tears that had their source in the remorse of Augustine, but only a basin that overflows, what separates these two countries is a notch of nothing, a stroke of two clock hours between neighbors, but to that is added our piles of filth, our ideas of separation, the murder that unites two brothers, all the dreams of murder that weave the anger of being solike-brothers who are so dissimilar, the mistrust that attaches their half-slumbers together.

BEFORE THE ORIGIN, THERE WAS PERHAPS A JARDIN D'ESSAI, THE PREHISTORY OF US, I THOUGHT, THE *PARDES* MY FRIEND JACQUES DERRIDA USED TO SAY TO ME, THE PASSAGE FROM 0 TO 1, FROM 1 TO 2, WITH SO MANY ORIGINS BETWEEN THE TWO, I SAY TO MY MOTHER, BEFORE THE CENTURY, AT THE DAWN OF THE CENTURIES, AT THE DAWN OF ALL THE CENTURIES,

THE JARDIN D'ESSAI BEFORE EVERYTHING, I SAY TO MY MOTHER,

OR THE TOMB, THE PASSAGE FROM ONE GARDEN TO ANOTHER.

THE JARDIN D'ESSAI BEFORE US,

I TRY TO GO THERE

BEFORE EVERYTHING

"Yesterday, I missed my entrance to the Jardin d'Essai." I am writing this to my friend J.D. The Jardin d'Essai, as people know somewhat since Jacques Derrida cultivated all its varieties in *H.C. for Life, That Is to Say* ceaselessly exercising his natural theoretical powers (of suggestion, seduction, sedition, sericulture), his natural allegorical, metaphorical, botanical, philological powers, thus his invisible, aerial and sublime, subterranean powers, both in conscious life and in the crypts of times difficult to reach, pasts and futures of the one and the other, I naturally went to the rendez-vous, the ultimate one, that is to say the one you gave me at the end of the publisher's insert, "*ultimate rendez-vous, in the Jardin d'Essai*" you said, the first rendez-vous at the Balzar, and the ultimate one in the Jardin d'Essai, "*at the intersection of paths to come*." You're always the one who picks the meeting places. I am writing this to J.D. I owe him an explanation. I am sitting at the window of the room in the Saint-Georges Hotel. From which saint am I going to ask for an explanation? I can't get over the fact that I didn't manage to enter. I don't have the time to think about this now. Now is the time for the confession, his naked face of a mocking angel. Is it a lapsus? What didn't I do? I can't prevent myself from comparing this failure, on the one hand to all the mythical failures, on the other hand to the victory that I took away the day before in El Biar, where I fought, and in totally unfavorable circumstances, but is that comparable?

At the beginning of the Test of El Biar, the sun had been up for about three hours, and at the end it is noon. I went from Obstacle to Refusal, by way of counterchauffeur – I am writing this to Jacques Derrida – following the directions your brother had given me when I was in France. Through the effect of pleasure and grief that takes hold of my power for living, the effect of the grief thus of the pleasure of tasting that special bitterness, my soul is completely gathered up in this power, that of living. So I was absorbed in the test. In another respect I was arguing at every turn up the hill with the counterchauffeur. – Take the Place d'El Biar, I say, go as far as the Cemetery. – There is no cemetery says the counterchauffeur. – Then I say Rue d'Aurelle de Paladines. – There is no Rue d'Aurelle de Paladines, says the other, no Paladines, I know El Biar he says. If I had had my Clos-Salembier body I would have followed my instinct, my body and I we would have wed ourselves to the curves, followed our noses on the roads, but I don't have an El Biar body, I have never gone there. I had your brother's words noted on a piece of paper and the images of your stories to guide me – I am writing this to Jacques Derrida. – You go to Birmandreis, you go up by way of the Petit Bois, you go down at Hydra, all this on foot or in the

129

car, says the counterchauffeur, but where you want to go man would have to fly. – Exactly, I say. Let us fly. I had the agile wings of the great desire of grief on the shoulders of my navy blue jacket. But not him. Right away on the left, Cemetery, two kilometers, second house, two stories, says your brother, my father had one story built and the second house is my parents', says your brother. No cemetery, that's a good start, that's a bad start says the counterchauffeur. Me with faith and hope crumpled on my shoulder blades. We climb up inside the split rock whose walls hugged us on each side. No cemetery? Oh! Everything became a cemetery for a quarter hour. Then when we were on top of the hill the Cemetery was there. As if I had come back to life. Go to the left, I say, I was following your stories, in a nameless street. There was, then, a street. How short the street was. We drove along it. Looking for the house, the villa. D'Aurelle de Paladines, I said. – Pizzeria says the counterchauffeur. No Aurelle no Paladines. Let's start again. "Christian Cemetery," closed, dead, but Cemetery, on the left, no, then on the right, image: you at the wheel car stolen from your father, shooting past, race car Chemin du Repos, driver, return. Still Pizzeria, no Aurelle, nowhere, the center. Christian Cemetery, I'm there. Let's start again. Facing the face of the Cemetery, with back to the Pizzeria, right, Rue Guynemer, sharp bend, Rue du Mont d'Or, with the mount of gold at the end, over there, you at the wheel of the car, at dawn when everyone is still asleep, before age fifteen, Rue Jean Jaurès, Chemin du Repos, no Aurelle, no villa, second story no. Once again, on foot, I was tired, all streets lead nowhere, lead back: Pizzeria. Standing with back to P. for Pizzeria, telephone your family, in vain the telephone rings, not surprised, in this kind of affair fate extends its lines and nets over the whole world. Chemin du Repos: a joke. Note: not a single shop, not a single passerby. deserted hypnotized streets, at the corners the fading signs with French names,

Guynemer! Jaurès! Help! Nobody. Not that I thought for one moment about the errancy of the letter, too tired, totally taken up with the search, not that I complained about an evil spirit or an evil eye, the car was not green, no rational explanation, irrational, superrational, I was there, Cemetery, and the street was not there. All the other streets. Strewn ruin. Purgatory, no not even. Antepurgatory. There: a gentleman, a lady, a car stopped, behind Cemetery. No Derrida, no Paladines, we don't know them. Close the trunk. Left. Later. – Drag yourself over here, Madame. A garage. With effort I came over to him on four paws. The men covered with grease, up to their neck in the pit so that I have their heads at my feet, don't know. Then out of her house came a well-dressed woman with a smooth white face around her blue Duchess of Guermantes eyes. Having been here a long time, I should know, she says, but never have I heard speak of any d'Aurelle de Paladines, nor Derrida, friendly, everything increases my pain, her patience, the calm blue of her eyes, her precision, her Italian silk scarf, next to her harmonious French mine crude, stumbling. Thus Daurelledepaladines, impossible, chimera! Faced with the friendly blue eye no idea, correctly, slowly vanquished. At my back: Pizzeria. "Let us go around again," the last time, I say to the counterchauffeur, and I hear myself speaking like the lady, with delicacy, roundedness, calm, a blue Guermantes speech. Exhausted, slowly convinced, convicted, condemned for an unknown long ago fault committed in France or in Algeria, by fault of being, neither Guermantes blue nor Kabyle blue, a fault too committed, forgotten, transmitted, by ancestors perhaps, for me to be able to disculpate myself. Nothing of everything that doesn't happen is taking place here and now I thought – I am writing all this to Jacques Derrida –

Surely I am hostage to one of those misunderstandings that poisoned my paths when I lived in Algeria, one last go-round, I will never forget this circular neighborhood that didn't give in to me, little by little one gets used up, one loses strength, confidence, luminosity, one bows down slowly before a face-less fate, even the sentences that so often escort me have nothing to say to me, they don't come in this neighborhood, the swifts have not followed me, the crow in the Cemetery croaks for nothing, I don't listen to it, it's over, I'm leaving. I make the round following the last round not in order to find, but to accustom myself to the decision I've made to give up. I have no wish to flee. I am waiting for the past to begin in five minutes at the corner of the Chemin du Repos.

And that's how I didn't find the house of my friend, I thought, despite and despite, who knows whom and what I obey, it's not the moment to think about that, I thought. These events have the consistency of shadows, and I will never come back.

Repentance has the hurried step of the young man who runs behind me. "Your last chance," he says. I have one foot in the car. "Madame, over there. Your last chance." I observe. A simple and eager face. A sentence lifted from a story whose beginnings he does not know. That gentleman over there: Your Last Chance. The eldest in the neighborhood. The Last Chance is thin. I hid nothing from him. In his turn he reveals. I am old, I alone know the secret passwords of the neighbor-hood, I am seventy years old, I live with my sister, I am the legend, he says. You are in the street that before was the street that you are looking for. At this very moment you are exactly where you cannot manage to find yourself. At that point the impossible cries out and disappears. He leads me through the same street, the street hidden in the street between the mask of the Cemetery and the Pizzeria. With his Roman head that rises living from the lifeless city, he leads us for thirty abandoned meters, to the corner that I passed by ten times. Pizzeria. Right here, my order is filled. Turn around! What are you doing? you're passing in front of the door with your back turned, look at it standing there, you will see the whole thing with the story that his father had built and whose front sticks out slightly over the high whitewashed walls. I was in front of your door, ten times I passed in front of the sober, high metal door, I didn't raise my eyes. But that's not it. The energetic and swift hands of my guide pressing on the shoulders of my navy blue jacket. The wings of pleasure and grief suddenly unfolded. You are there. And the door was green. That's it. I passed in front of the door, it was green, I couldn't stop. Seeing green [*le vert*] is not in your tradition, seeing the worm [*le ver*], that's your tradition. A green door must remain closed. I was in front of your door. To its right, Pizzeria.

O sublime virtue, desire for resurrection, that led me by the cunning circles of the unconscious, around in front of the tombs whose covers gaped, how much blindness had to mature in my eyes, numerous and subtle are the ways of resisting the narrow little streets in which I have to weave before arriving, an hour after the end, right after Pizzeria, in front of the green door of the apocalypse There is nothing and there is not nothing. The house is sober. Surrounded by all the depths. The cemetery is so close.

When he steals his father's car, before any license, before the sun, he speeds in front of the home of death, around the world in five minutes, at the other end of the world smolders the mount of gold of the moon, the beginning is very close to the end in the final turn begins the beginning, the whole world and its universes are contained in this crisp perimeter enclosed by walls and not one meter and not one cat that is not the secret servant of philosophy.

I thought that I wouldn't find The House.

I struck the rock twice. I went round the neighborhood seven times and an eighth time. In the end Monsieur Mohamed came out to buy bread for his sister. I doubt myself, I doubt doubt.

133

I came to this country of Algeria where I was born and each time I sought an entrance I found myself losing my way in the wings of the theater in Oran, for that's where doubt and losing my way began when I was five years old, it's still as if I were in the place of me, as if I were passing too soon in front me, running, I didn't speak the tongue of my mouth, I took a stranger for my mother and I took my mother for another, I was not with me, and, finally, I wrote, to J.D., I went to the Jardin d'Essai rendez-vous hurriedly, as if I had opened your book, without thinking.

I don't have time to think about it now. I saw the Garden – from the heights of the Chemin des Crêtes, from the *lycée* I saw the brilliant greens rolling down toward the sea from the parapets, it's all one sees, its palaces of overpopulated foliage from the haunted pages of its former wild animals, from very far from very high from the photo albums that try to imitate it, from the pasts perched at my sides, from the city of Oran where my father promised us in 1946 the Paradise *d'essai*, from 1947 when Papa took us as soon as we moved into Clos-Salembier from the heights, in a rapid, exalted cortege, as far as the adorable one, in greens fitted with corks and scales all the way to the lane of carnivorous plants that Papa lightly brushed says my brother, to make their alligator jaws move, and then later without Papa, without the sublime charmer I saw the hell of paradise, the cruel beauty of the *jardin décès*, the death garden, its offensive and gentle indifference, a carnivore of ground-up joys, the versatility of its fidelity and later I lived, my brother with me like a single child, the reconquest of the Garden but the barefoot hermaphrodite that we were lingered no longer at the delights, shehe with indeterminate face but decisive heart crosses at a tireless run the Garden metamorphosed into a forest for the dead so as to go jump in the water of the municipal pool. Since unfortunately it is freezing the joy of calming the fever soon turns into painful shivers. In vain we tried to keep happiness, first one dies from the heat then one dies from the cold

The test is over. I never doubted the Jardin d'Essai. I never tamed the Jardin d'Essai. I myself have changed its immense powers of metamorphoses into a fable. An insurrectional fluid is mixed up with its sap. There exist only five gardens in the world that are so bewitching. Certain species secrete forgetfulness. Others the unforgettable, with the peppery scent of the terebinth. To *the ultimate rendez-vous* at the intersection of paths to come where we have never been together separately I will go then, one alone for both of us. Wahib is driving Zohra's car each time naturally we have to go all the way round the city so as not to enter by the main gate for the main characters are not the ones you think, the main gates are there to put you off the scent, it's by the hidden gate that one can slip into the supernatural. When one stands before the Entrance of the Essai it can only be the other one. One wants to go quickly, it can only be very slow.

I was there. I am standing before the secondary gate. I have my papers, my passport. The high dull fences. One does not enter. Naturally I don't believe that. I am already in a supernatural dream deep within the lane of the giant ficus trees, I will go to the baobabs, at the sight of my father in an almost white suit, my tears will gush, I am trembling. They do not let me enter. I shouldn't tell you this, murmurs J.D. but you ought to have made inquiries already several days ago he says, and I read the slight annoyance of reproach in that revered voice. There, now I've said what I promised myself I wouldn't say. You should have thought of it earlier says the revered voice. I should have thought of it earlier. What is meant by "to believe," "to be able," "to regret" "too late," the eternal altercation starts up again, and I alone am there to be guilty, I live to answer for the fault, and to live is a fault for which I can ask forgiveness from no one. I am standing in reality before the secondary gate therefore the main gate of the story and the Garden is closed for five years. No use trying. The police is sitting in the garden on the steps of the white sentry box it is smoking and doesn't hear my condemned person's moan. J.D. reminds me of what was for forty years our friendship and you usually so organized, you think of everything and finally you think of nothing says the revered voice. I think nothing. What else but nothing does the condemned one think when standing before the execution apparatus? Because if I had thought to ask the all-powerful Zohra that a pass, a grace, be granted to me. I think nothing. My unconscious likewise. My whole internal space is taken up by the bars. You wished it. You did not wish it. And do I know? Behind me Monsieur Wahib. The enormous gate is padlocked in reality, I recognize it I recognize the coat of arms of my destiny. By what right did I forget that I didn't have the right? I was born with Garden Forbidden. Nothing changes. For his part Monsieur Wahib does not give in, he was also born with his destiny. I am jealous of a seagull that enters the Garden though the air. Monsieur Wahib parleys with the guardian of the other side. The law applied to my dreams for the last five thousand years: "Who wishes to enter will not enter. And it will be her fault." Monsieur Wahib's law is his honor in the struggle for life. It's closed for five years. But for five minutes, between Monsieur Wahib on his side and the guardian on the other side, a possibility opens up that doesn't belong to the ethical order, that is neither proscribed nor forbidden that is not a permission or an authorization, that is the duration of a mystical hospitality. Five minutes says Wahib. The guardian says: *Rapidman*, quickly. Rapidman: the heart's talisman. I don't believe it but to hell with belief. Take the world Rapidman. Rapidman. Like three accomplices before the garden of desires Monsieur Wahib the guardian and I pledge an oath. Rapidman: I swear it.

"Rapidly" the guardian is thus on your side, rapidman that is to say *too quickly*, the theme of the quarrel that never gave us any respite, here we are clinging to the bars you with the guardian by your side you say to me: "*I told you and I tell you again that life will have been short and here I am recalling once again that in the end too quick*" – I know, I know, I thought but I say nothing, I have never in my life interrupted your thought, meanwhile I beg Wahib to beg the guardian on your side, open, open, I know, I know, that every minute is a year and every year a life, the miracle, for I insist on believing that it's indeed a miracle, is that the gate is open a crack. So we rush forward. Rapidman! yells the guardian on his side. So we run into the path of the dracenas. Rapidman! So we run into the arms of the first tree we come to, this dracena with nine arms that it spreads for me. Rapidman.

Already we feel the leash, for we are dogs.

Rapidman is finished! *One* dracena! Done! Short, you were right. But all the same I touched the sky. One has to invent the speed that rapidly changes rapidman time into stretches of eternities. I don't have the time to feel bad this morning. And that's good. "I missed well and good the Jardin d'Essai." I write that. And it's good. I don't have the time to think about it.

I wrote this letter to J.D. and I mailed it from the Casbah in the broken letters box. Smashed jaw. Eat my letter. Skeleton. How human was its face of a toothless old beggarwoman, may no one ever chase her away.

If mybrother-who-is-not-with-me returns on his side the gates will not be open or closed, closed although open, secondary thus principal destinal like they are for me but mybrother will not return

he did not come with me,
there were apparent impediments
I went alone and by half
With the benediction of the dead,
The living have spectralized me
Please tell me how I can get into 54 Rue Philippe in
Oran
With mybrother lacking, without legs, without feet to feel
the floor of the shadowy entryway, without hands to feel in
the dark the place of the staircase where the polished wood
railing is
there is no railing, there are no wooden steps
with one eye closed and one ear cut off
that's what, because of mybrother, I am obli
at the last mi
he refu
because there are places where I am not half mybrother
but 54 Rue Phil
without bro

I didn't want to go up, it was not me, there was no staircase,
there was no railing, there was no entryway, there was no door
to the street, it's Sid Ahmed who pushed me, I stepped back,
I was on the sidewalk in front of the house, an old woman
came out of the nothingness at number 54, a faded flower,
I'm afraid of falling, at the end of the hallway into the hole
of memory, to the right beneath the staircase the abode of
Mohamed I don't see it, there is no closet, there is no continuation of the story, there is no time, instead of my brother I
struck up a friendship the day before with Belkhacem and thus
with Sid and right away 54 Rue Philippe I share the memory
withmybrother with them, they were not born in 54, but for
54 it is I who am not there this year, I clearly saw in the dark
that I was going to kill, I said no no no. What? Kill the world,

no, kill my father and my mother, go up go up, no no, kill my brother and my grandmother, the last hour of 54, no no, kill the neighbor across the hall and *le dindon dodu d'Adidas le dentiste*, the plump turkey cock of Adidas the dentist, give me your hand, no no, I'm afraid, I said that no: I'm afraid I should not have said it, it's not fear, it's the explosion of the world I mean to say mow down a life in five steps fifty years no that's not it, exchange the pearly eternity of this realm that remains lit up, no, behind my thought for a plate of lentils, to cut the thread of the planet that governs my dreams with a stroke of the scissors, I was hospitalized in a library, no, no no I don't want anyone to grab the lamp away from me, I was struggling according to my friends, just a few steps, call me a coward, I say let me run away, and you you weren't with me mybrother to share the fright. No.

One mustn't kill a city that lays golden eggs, the whole golden family and all the books, drop this knife. But what am I doing there my god, hospitalized by mistake in my bookshelves? The old lady said we could go up. After the darkness the day would begin again on the first floor.

Now, it's done. Do you want to keep it? We'll wrap it for you. They wrap my dead lamp in the pages of the *Echo d'Oran*.

If I don't answer it's because of the molten blood my mouth is full of lentils that swim in a gush of blood. From the balcony I say to my brother on the telephone, across the street there is no longer the plump turkey cock of Adidas, but still the superb view on the square. The family is well, father, mother, grandmother, two little ones. How do you spell Cixous? B-e-n-a-o-u-f, I say.

– The death of some Oranais poultry is not so terrible, it's life.

– We'll talk about it again in fifty years.

But to come back down the steep cement incline that used to be the wooden staircase in the old days Sid Ahmed holds me back by the hand while I slip into the mute throat and I'm amazed at the thoughtfulness of fate that copies exactly the characters of one family from the other, the Kabyle version of Omi my German grandmother is so perfectly translated that I forgot in the kitchen, where the grandmother in Omi's place offers me pastries, that I am the same age in Oran as my German grandmother who now has for a successor the Kablye grandmother and for five minutes with my mouth filled with honey I am five years old and a double grandmother. "When you return," said the Kabyle version with the green eyes of my father's Kabyle eyes. But the anesthesia wears off and I find myself again Rue Philippe I wake up while rapidly losing the taste of the dream of transposition. What is found in its place is delicious, but it's what has been lost that exerts the most powerfully inexhaustible charm. Will I also lose the Benaouf period one day? But the melancholic headiness is granted to mortals only after the end of the end. In forty years decomposition will no doubt have overtaken not only the staircase but still other organs of the building's old body, and on this subject Monsieur Benaouf and I agree for one does not kill Rue Philippe one lets die.

And to try to save what is going to disappear in a future with an indecipherable face, of enigmatic age, perhaps tomorrow already at the latest next week, I run to write you a letter that will begin with these words: "My love, I am trembling so much I can't write with my hand . . ." to Rue Bagdadi Mohamed, the street of the public scribes. I am sitting on a tiny yellow stool on the sidewalk next to one of the five public scribes sitting one after the other, open to uncertainty, veteran companions of Thot brought down into the street by the series of wars, the

140

second of the resigned cohort, to whom blind choice has led me. For they are all sitting equally daydreaming with a typewriter grafted onto their bent knees. Some secret order was given to me to crouch next to Hassan Naso, outlawed public scribe, the handsome man with moist eyes.

Hassan: – What is the aim?

H. – So as not to forget. (The scribe types severely. Is it a letter?)

Him. – Love?

H. – Yes.

Him. – Roman letters. (He is a master, I dictate to him what he dictates to me.) He is in a foreign land? I say yes, a foreign land, a strange land. Stranger in a strange land. Yes. Him: The address, please. H.: 54 Rue Philippe in Oran. He will understand. Him: "My love." He precedes me and he passes me. "We are separated," he types. No, I say, "we do not leave each other," "love is a river," he types, then the river overflows "Rue Philippe still runs to the sea, as you know even if my hand is trembling, LOVE, types Hassan, CAPITALS ON DEEP FEELINGS LIKE THE WATER OF THE RIVER AND SOMETIMES LIKE THE OCEAN OF THE PLANET, ALSO LOVE IS STRONG LIKE DEATH, IF YOU ARE IN A FOREIGN LAND THE FOREIGNER IS YOURS, YOU KNOW WHERE TO FIND ME, that's enough I say, it's good as it is, who do I sign? says Hassan, *H.* for *G.*, I say. He types *J*. I say: no, *G.* He types "J. like Juliet." There. But I say this letter is a river and you are its author, please sign your writing. He signs: "Love has deeper feelings than we do. The times are come. This expression as a token of peace and love from a public scribe," signed Hassan of Oran the outlawed poet,

who recommends that you love one's neighbor in the love of god who recommends that you do not kill god with religious blows. For I warn you Israelis and Palestinians are going to be reconciled. All those who have the power of presidents and popes will not succeed in separating them.

141

Myself, I was ripped off. I was formed by the mounted police of Francis I and chased away by the mounted police. What escaped was the other feeling I had. It's not the anti-love presidents and popes that speak to me of the foreigner, the stranger, but things beings come from the heights of antiquity and that have not yet departed. I am not the slave of religion, I am not the slave of culture or wars piece by piece I am the slave of the love of God the neighbor who will come later hoping that all will not have been destroyed. I shave myself, the mirror is the sky, god shaves himself in front of the mirror.

Certain people say that every bullet has its ticket, ticket that's passport with visa so as to have the freedom to go from one country that doesn't want you to a country that doesn't want you. But the master of my ticket is love. Love, that's the remedy, says he, Hassan the outlawed poet.

The letter is now fifty pages long. He doesn't want to be paid because (1) peace has no price, (2) he is my brother I am his sister. When I call him from Paris no one answers at the number he gave me, it's as if he gave me god's number. Often I dial the number, I call, I remember, I can't forget the outlaw who prophesied to me in Rue Bagdadi Mohamed. This street exists in reality. How did they meet? How to explain the fact that he read what the other would have wanted to think in her own thought? Where did the sentences come from? Whispered to which unconscious, stolen from which unconscious? There is all the love and all the pain of the world in the letter, all the genius of pain and the madness of love in French but the soul of the work is foreign.

A donkey! I cried. If there must be a relation between Hassan the outlawed poet and the donkey, at the moment I see the Donkey I was not thinking of it. There was the donkey.

He crossed in front of me in Rue Bagdadi Mohamed. His immortal little trot. And it could only be the Donkey. No other. Not one donkey anywhere. I run. The donkey-driver hurries the donkey. I cry out briefly Donkey! Donkey! but what? The donkey-driver or the donkey, I don't know, runs away. Disappears at the end of the street. The only donkey in Oran. I pleaded for it, I chased it away. The outlaw flees. It was. You thought it was a cat, says Sid Ahmed. Eurydice, I say. The soul of Oran. Myself I cause my loss

My mother reads the long letter at length. This one is inspired, possessed by peace. He's an envoy of God for peace in the world. Don't telephone him, you will never find a way out of it, there will never be peace. He's a born poet but ill-born. I found only one mistake. There is a French mistake. There are not a lot because there is only one. Poor unknown poet says my mother. – You see what good it is? – What? – Poetry.

Why in order to write a posthumous letter to G. in a foreign land did I need the translation of my being by a public street scribe in Oran? I wanted to say to you "my love all is lost nothing is lost," instead of me I needed Homer Hassan and his dog to write in capital letters, I clung to the rock wandering in this still vociferating century. This giant atom, an invention of Oran, teaching passers-by to love the animal warmth of Peace, was there, at the hour of my despair, with two white envelopes, all that he had left and all of literature. To crouch at Homer's side, a stone's throw from the Lycée that was Lamoricière and has resuscitated all yellow as Pasteur, is to obey the literary premonition of literature. Already in Oran, when I was five years old, G. my father, the war, the expulsion, the Vichy viper, I hoped without having ever heard speak of – even

143

his name did not grow in the middle of the whistled hatreds and panicky cries of the sirens – for a Homer or another Ovid necessary for the salvation of children. Literature is the absolute being sitting against the wall of the house beside the lemonade-seller's shop in the Oran street that preserves in a meter and a half square the archives written in free verse of all the proscriptions of the proscribed suffering from triumphs. And the literary miracle is that I really found the one I was not looking for, whom I didn't think I was looking for in Oran

He sends me postcards. *Sister Hélène Cixous Paris Your brother and friend Hassan is thinking of you Poste Restante Oran.* Two twenty-dinar stamps on the envelope. The stamp represents the scene in Rue Bagdadi Mohamed. In the foreground the writer is occupied writing with a quill in a schoolboy's notebook. Behind him the woman dictates the letter that the writer in truth dictates to her. He is wearing a navy blue shirt. I am wearing a yellow blouse.

In vain I write to him Hassan O. Naso poste restante R/P Oran. Finally I write ALGERIA Poste Restante Oran. But no one knows why the TRISTIA are returned to sender. I am sure I met him in reality

– Where are you?

He rises. It's my Thursday. He is beautiful like "The Day" and that is what he is. He comes streaming out of the rosy golds of Algiers. I am mortally happy, for he is the adored one the terrible one the one who comes only once. He gives time, he takes time back. I dress quickly while keeping my eyes on the sky that counts pulsations in colors.

– Where are you?

You see, your adored voice would kill me with joy if I had not sworn to live Today.

– I am very close by, I say, at the Saint-Georges Hotel. Where you have never been I believe. And I add: because of the name. As if you didn't know. It's because our Absolute familiarity is so mad that I mumble reasons.

– But yes I was, yes. – Yes? I say. – I was there, a long time ago. – You were here? You have been here? But it's not the moment to talk about the hotel. The car is waiting for me. I say: "to Saint-Eugène." We are surrounded by saints, I thought. I am going to my saint. I have left the city. We arrive quickly at the edge of the world. There the difficulties begin and thus the hysterical anxieties because of the blessed cruelty of this expected happiness. Infinite I am finite. He is The Day, he is everything, there is only one. The problem is that the entrance to the cemetery is sealed off. That's the first problem. Then will come the various attempts to get around the obstacle by all sorts of clever ideas, aborted. All the same I will not complain because every pain is vivid like love and every powerlessness is the broken wing of a power whose injuring I bless. While I am guided by the saints I am

145

surrounded by a choir of the curious, men and women from the city, workmen, employees, ditchdiggers, unemployed, guardians distracted by my passage. I am the unhoped-for interruption of boredom and idleness. It's not their fault that I want to remain in my secret glory even if, when I drag them behind me like a swarm of realities, onlookers buzzing among the gods, I call down on their heads a hail storm, it's my fault because I recognize their rights as provisional victors not to be obliged to suffer in advance what will happen when they are no long standing and kicking the bones of the tombs and picking their teeth with twigs from the bushes. It's not their fault if the holiday for me is on your side, vanity on their side, for they are everybody according to whom you are nothing.

To enter the Jewish cemetery whose gate is closed, several solutions. One can make a hole underground and crawl, with the drawbacks you can imagine. I thought of using the tidal wave. I let myself fall into the narrow gorge carved out between the small red cliffs. But once down there in the humid cell I said to myself that this is madly reckless, I feared that by plunging down the hole the water instead of lifting me to the heights might drown me. I decide to go back up the rock that is the height of my shoulders. There begins my terrible powerlessness. Others than myself would have done it quickly. I make superhuman efforts and for nothing. It's my paralysis as always. The soul lifts off, the body rests below. I am half-emerged my head against the face of the rock, my legs don't follow. There are a bunch of people sitting. They watch me doing my best. They are waiting for me to finish. I take one of my legs in both hands and I try desperately to lift it. It's acrobatic. The secretary, a very young girl, says to me: my poor dear, you are split in two. – It's a matter of right, I have the desire but I lack the right, I want to say that, I think I have the right to cut short the ordeals, my soul wants to believe that

146

I've paid and waited enough, but my body doesn't support me, not yet, a profound unbelief saws me off at the waist, a part of me, when I affirm that there is not death where one believes, believes me, at the same time my lower limbs cancel me out, I know this paralysis, it surges up against me every time I am very close to succeeding in cutting short the death penalty. So I want to say. I could say a lot on the subject. But not a single word escapes suffocation. All the force of my thought united to my passion, to the pride of my desire, to my conviction that I am very close, so close to the goal of my life, don't tip the balance. I remain thus. Until total exhaustion. I can't do like everyone else. Yet time hurries on. In the end I stopped struggling against myself. I sat down on the ground at the foot of the wall, I took my deepest slowest longest maturing interior running start, I began to lift the world and myself, and I came out of the self-enslavement. I wanted to go the quick way around, but it backfired on me to have been so hasty in my desires. So I change horizons. I decide on the pre-entrance. Another solution, which is to go by way of the Catholic entrance. One penetrates without visible obstacle, then it's just a matter of the unconscious and discretion. I walk slowly and fast, between the Catholic graves that I mingle with as little as possible, I don't want to take advantage of their time and their faith but I also don't want to grant any more to Rome than, by the force of circumstances, I must. I go on for a long time like this, I recognize it, this realm is extraordinarily spread out, and while making my way I muse about these juxtapositions, these cave-ins of time, these battles of worlds, these roarings of centuries that continue underground with the effect that my passage, which is careful of ancient sensitivities, thus neither too slow which would be offensive nor too rapid, which would be insulting, is accompanied by a perpetual roll of underground thunder. I pass by. I go back through the history of the Church and the history of Empires

147

People believe that everything is dead and that it's peace, but they're wrong, all the weapons are not laid down, some are regrouped in military formation, lined up enlisted the sword brandished for the war that never lets up.

No one knows what a tomb is.

Behind me meanwhile the choir follows its other ideas. In every regard my curious Centaurs are on their ground, I hear it in their autochthonous speech. Here is not their death. Here is not death for my Centaurs. Here is foreign death.

Lively conversation behind me, the way the nurses in the emergency room weave their birds' nests above the agonizing ones who are leaving with their last good-byes, what they ate, what they saw at the movies, the weather, the times, those that flutter toward the beautiful continents, those that are contained in a jar where the last drop is hidden. No relation. The times do not meet up in Emergencies. It's at what time, lunch? And still ten thousand lunches. I'm afraid that they will kill my sadness, don't touch me!

Today, no one else in the long garden of the separated ones, no one crosses the years, except for the choir and me. A dozen pass by seemingly without trembling. But who knows what they dreamt last night? No one knows what death murmurs to the seemingly living. Without warning, one passes, one is past. Like from the Catholics to the Jews, without passage, without passing, among the yews and the cypresses the same ones the ground the same as itself, without having realized it I have already been among the Jews for some time, there is no gate, no ditch, when one was going to die perhaps one didn't notice that one had passed to the other side, one was dead and one didn't know it before a little while and perhaps never or else one still lives, the trees are the same, and the love and the pain, only the rhythms of the times are totally out of joint.

Moving away from the choir the guardian goes in front of me. – The address? – Never any address I say. That's the

principle of this book. Tomb without address. On top of
the hill, I say. It was on top of the hill when we climbed my
brother and I, for not only did you have to go to death but
what's more you had to go up there very high over and above
our strength beneath the sky, before giving up.

Next I
cut myself
off from myself
myself
my tomb
from my tomb
stopped
I stopped   my tomb   my title
of pain
stopped

where did it go? The pain? The signature, the tomb?
The number? We will see, yells the guardian. Is it in the
register? yells the guardian. Yells. It's because something like
an abyss prevents me from going as far as the registry office.
Is it outside the text? Does it hold me outside the text?

– You will not find it, says my mother.

Someone yells. What is his name? says the yell. And I like
a damned one I yell: Cixous. I am thunderstruck. Here I hear
my voice yelling Cixous. I throw the stone at myself. Cixous
what? Then my voice is yelling: Cixous Georges. As if you
were dead. As if I were speaking of you. As if I were saying
bad things about you in front of you. Never have I committed
that. *Cixous Georges*, screams the choir, and I am the choirmas-
ter. Never will I be able to forgive this blasphemy. Now I am
going to have to eat the burning coals to the very last one.

– *Do you know the date?* yells the yell. I will not answer. Before
me silence is cut to pieces and blood streams on my cheeks.

– The date! The date! yells the guardian. And I drag the
date from my heart. I admit. I confess your death. I make

resound in the empty, devouring air the secret of your death. This date is my cipher, my key, it's my record, no one knew it exactly, my record, my judgment, my condemnation, it's my ring of eternity, I never exchanged it except with the unique one, I hid it in my books beneath decoys, in forgeries, invoking it and sealing it caressing it beneath the veil, calling it to my aid, only the moon knew it, the unique one, here I go and give it up, I yell it at the top of my lungs, I spit out the bits of heart into the mouth of the void. I thus came all the way here to slit my lamb's throat. I want to die then, altogether, right away.

But you remain unlocatable in the register and I don't go near it: I'm afraid they will kill my sad joy. I stopped before a tomb. I lower my eyes. *Eugène Derrida*. That's the title.

This whole scene will take place outside the book, I say to myself, it doesn't belong to the same search.

It's here that I plunge beyond the babble of the choir of centaurs and prophecies.

– You'll see nothing. It's all overgrown.

– There's nobody who has that name on that date.

I say to those who have followed me: don't follow me! The guardian comes up, how to prevent him? In the middle of the path of death stands a large yellow thing, a cross between a building and a petrified lion. I say that It was not there when I came in the past. He says that it has always been there: this is where the Jews wash the dead. Since there have been dead the yellow washhouse has been there, he's surely right in his knowledge. But in my just madness there was no yellow rock to obstruct my ascent. And with a beating of the wing I am further away.

Don't follow me! I didn't bring the pruning shears, if I have to I'll cut the underbrush with my teeth, but there is no underbrush, I climb on the driving force of pain, it has waited so long for bliss, it forms now its flood by increasing toward the heights, the squares of decimated tombs see us pass. The man is hunting in front of me, ferreting, I say: it's red granite, I don't know what that means it's what we used to say so as not to say the false truth, the horror, very simple I say, and he goes off sniffing among the monuments. Then it's higher up, surely higher than higher. Where are you? I am listening to you my love, oh, I am listening to you and I hear you, because our supernatural telephone is now plugged in, the whole mountain quakes with your murmur. – Where are you? I say quickly, anguished, I want your speech to guide me, where are you? – *So close.* Oh the delicious pain of hearing your breath once more familiar, so close. I was so close, I didn't see you, where are you? I said these words toward the top of the hill, I didn't dare cry out, the slumber of these sleepers seemed so fragile to me, I murmured loudly Where are you? as if you alone could hear me and in fact I heard you answer me: *are you?* I climbed toward the echo. "Where are you" I called out at the corner of block 39 I was sure that you were not far. ". . . are you?" I went higher, I was wearing white tennis shoes, shards of the gravestones rolled beneath my soles, "you are there?" I whispered, I was at the angle of 40 – "there!" Very sharply in my eyes I had the image of your feet wearing white tennis shoes in 1942, I didn't do it on purpose, "Higher?" I crossed an edge of crumbling wall. "Higher?" No more echo and I didn't dare pitch my voice louder. I was wringing my heart. It occurred to me that I might have passed you by and not seen you, perhaps all the misfortune of my life has been to pass *very close and perhaps so close* to the face of happiness that I don't see it and perhaps having always been so close to seeing my life is my fate, of being perhaps two meters away from you, my whole life two steps away, you have already passed by, I was standing at the western corner of block 41, I could no longer hear and I could no longer see. All the sharp blue of the sky fell into my eyes. To the left of the blue a green needle planted in the belly of the sky.

I sat down on the ground in the alleyway of Clos-Salembier in front of the closed gate, you had just left, I was calling out, I set the word Papa in front of me and I watered it with a stream of tears.

The man in 2006 over there cries: it's here! I say to the men: leave me. I say to those who are talking loud and not murmuring: "Go no further! Go away!" I want your voice, my love, speak once more, pour me once again the mad draft of immortality. "*So close!*" how you sing, and to find once again the laughter, the freshness, the dew, that way you have of moistening words, of silvering them to make them shine, that accent of mockery. You always made fun of me, you loved me and led me with mockery, I was blind so you would light my way, I stumbled so that you would hold me up with your slender and firm hand, in this very moment I see nothing, and I hear you laughing at me, at my fever, my panic, as in the past, as always, as usual, you are just, beside me, just beside me, around me everywhere the teeth of the shattered, beaten-down tombs, gaping jaws, scattered jewels, I rest my hand on the tree. And you are there. At the cypress.

How small you are, my love, my little one. You seemed so big in the past too big, too heavy, too dead, you were angry perhaps, with us the children who did not come to open the gate, who fled before the appearance, who didn't have the idea that is to say the courage the sense to break down the wall, who did not hold your hand, unearth you, who howled a bitter laugh behind the neighboring monument while Mémé your mother wept big tears on your stone, we feared you, beloved, I was afraid of your bones I feared the worms, I wanted to leave, I left, I left you, I let you fall into solitude, where there was never forgetfulness. I remember the very severe being you seemed to me to be, I swallowed my shame and my terror behind your head and I saw your arrival in the cemetery, your condemned man's arrival, in a light-colored suit, I saw you

152

pass among the cypresses, with your eyes so close to green a little yellow, in which I saw by the yellow gaze that read me that they saw everything. And to have seen you so little and lived you so intensely and wanted you so passionately had left you immense, in the abandoned state, in this unvisited hall of Saint-Eugène. And to have known you too late after your withdrawal, to have loved you too late and slowly thought your being at its height, to have met you by chance and found you by pieces, to have found so late the secret in suffering and that the dead who make us suffer are living. Until all the meaning of what remained for me to live turned in the direction of the Algeria to which I had left you. In the end your apparition measured as large as the ground where I had bequeathed you to a limitless solitude. Such an abandonment had spread in me. I was sheltering the unforgotten.

Near the cypress I find myself, me who was at a loss for you, and I find you as if I was finally finding sight, the precise truth the precise-making truth of which I was deprived, in the startling second of the apocalypse I see true and I see that I see: *how small you are*, how simple you are, how well-formed you are, how you are. What happens to me: seeing at last your immortality, and it is so small. During thirty-nine years, I was not here. Your thirty-nine-year-old death, your thirty-nine-year-old life. I went to revive pain on contact with your face, I say to myself. I could no longer bear to be separated from it. I was suffering from running dry. I was thirsty.

You are safe and sound. All the others damaged. In front of you a disemboweled, eviscerated, pillaged tomb. To your right one that had been a tomb, crumbled into a hundred pieces of debris. You alone clean, condensed, essence of immortality. And I was alone with you. I had not asked for that. I could never have wished for this solitude. I had never been absolutely alone with you. All my life with you

153

shared with my brother. Never could I have wished for such a sovereign solitude. It was yourself, sober. The economy of your elegance. My reserved, pensive wild animal. On your slightly squared shoulders, from this distance, under the water of light poured by the cypress they were as if moistened by a sweat of dew, your fine head turned toward a future that I did not see as if to show me with a lifting of your chin the direction of your reverie, from this I saw that I was lying on your bed, and that the inaccessible was granted to me.

I see That – but from the other side. I see everything from the other side, as in the beyond-life, beyond-memory

My brother is not there. I embraced you. I lay down upon you. I fastened myself with all my strength to the Tomb I felt how living it was, its hardness supple at my call, I caressed my father's forehead and I spoke to you, with the gentle authority of faith that acts at will. There is nothing more, says my mother. Except for the rest I say. In the past I used to be afraid of teeth. Fear of the rest. That death had set its teeth against me and reciprocally fear of having set my teeth against death. I had not yet found the strength of conversion. Today I know how to put back together again. All I need is a hair, a tooth. I lost a flood of tears. Yet I didn't want to lose anything. With a wet handkerchief I washed your skin. I couldn't have done better. Sin to throw away one's tears. Sin to wash your granite except with tears. Your red dust. I wept. I prolonged the ablution beyond. You were looking at me. I saw beyond my gaze your almost lowered eyelids, I saw the dream of your gaze through the slits of your eyelids, a gaze in a strange, sweet and interminable dream which doesn't see like the eyes of this world see which sees something that I cannot see with my eyes but whose reflection I see in the motionless silk of your pupils and since it shines without moving I believe it is eternity. Then I felt under my fingers the return of the living feeling for

154

the first time of your shiny black hair that gave you a disobedient wing. Youremember the net? What a violent naïveté! On these hasty, wild curls, which gave you the crown of an incorrigible angel, they crushed the mesh of a black net.

I was lying on you, I called.

Everyone can call. It suffices *to be able*. That is to say. It suffices to be able to be able. It suffices to be able to want to be able. Myself I had never been able to want to be able, it was the first time. This kind of superpower without will propelled purely by a well-given wanting cannot be directed, nor commanded, nor practiced at regular intervals, it is neither a cult, nor a rite, nor a spiritual exercise, it is not even a grace, it is a chance, set loose by a miraculous conjunction of accidents some external and others internal, like a sublime error, from strict heavenly tabulation, it cannot be caused, it can only be received and then lingers only to the extent of the strength of the subject's superhuman exaltation.

I should have been with my brother according to law and destiny. According to a counter-destiny I was not with my brother. I am so close. One cannot be any closer. I put my lips to this page. I lowered my eyelids. Don't touch us, anyone! You are in me. I called. With my voice I hollowed out the stone in me, I opened up the ground, with my body, I called your body, with my body I saw your whole body, I lifted you and you got up carefully. – You're alone, there? I said yes. I passionately wanted to hear your voice, that it be you who speaks and I who carry. But I cleaved to your signs I guessed the effort such an emersion cost someone exhausted by death. – I want to embrace you I know it is not the time, I say. – Yes it is, yes, it's time, you say, and I gather up tenfold the delicate but clear inflexions of your voice. – It's time? – Yes, yes. – Describe how you are, there, you say. I notice that you say *there* several times, it's because you haven't got your sight. I don't have time to think about that here. – Kneeling

155

a little – I say. Leaning over you but without weighing down. – Dressed? – Dressed? Black slacks, a white blouse with blue stripes. I think ardently: and you? But I didn't dare. I will ask my brother to describe you. If any bones remain. But I dare to desire what I desire. – I want to take you in my arms and devour you. – Devour, you say. Come. With each word, with each second my heart spurts a triumph of joy, I was afraid of the joy, that it might make me stagger.

Come and *being* were mingled. I gave him my being so that he might be. And during this whole time without limits I was pushing the limit back, and during this time without limits there was no going no coming no future no conditional, and during this whole time I was resisting the end that would come, and there was no end in the conversation.

– I am writing a text that is completely traversed by you, I say, even if it seems to be by someone other than you. – I'm used to that. – To what? – To being replaced.

Right then I was seized by an immense tenderness and I recognized the annunciation of pity. I sensed that the blood of the call was running out. I called him my child. I said, my child, you are my child, you know? – I know, I know.

And with the word *know* I set him back down.

I called my brother. I am with Papa. He is moved. My brother. My father. He is there, I say. – What do I say to him? I say. – Tell him that he is not forgotten. Says my brother who is not here, who does not see me. Does not see that I am sitting on Papa. I telephone him. Lying at his side.

– I am putting on the speaker I say. The voice of my brother lands on the tomb. Tell him that he has great influence on our lives, that he is blessed. The voice deep, slow, deeply slowly, comes, heavy, timid, light. – I have put your voice upon him, I say.

I call my mother – Ah! you found? – I found, I say.

I found: the absolute construction. We have found the absolute, I say to myself. But for my mother the important thing is not the object, it's the finding. Whereas for me it's the non-named, the secret, the adorable, that is essential.

– What shall I say to him? I say. She says: – Poor dear! He did not have the chance to live enough to see what followed. Are you going elsewhere now, my darling?

My mother says: he. She says: you.

I go elsewhere

– I'm going to the Clinic, Maman dear. I am going to the Clinic d'Isly, to my mother's castle of life, in the book of the everyday. I am returning to life, I say. She says: if you return to the city stop at the Fish Market. And I go there.

– The grouper is better if it's fresh, says my mother.

It is noon.

She did the right thing by entrusting him to the chest of red granite, the smallest volume, without commentary, a nontomb, all around the high and heavy tombs with clumsy apostrophes have succumbed. Except my father who is safe.

And what if you had been wounded, my tomb, chipped, scratched, collapsed, my heart, my beauty?

My mother put us away in a solidly made drawer and we held up.

– You will not find it, said my mother.

I believed her without believing her.

What the camera does not see.

It did not see me embrace you, wipe the dust off your granite face with my tears

157

– I couldn't bear to see Mémé lie down on the tomb said my brother. When she sat on Papa her enormous wild animal body enraged by death, when she hurled her lengthy roars, when she gave birth to her dead one by releasing bloody urine over the whole earth, I couldn't bear it. Now if I were alone I would do it, I believe that I would do it.

One wants to be alone in the chamber
For this love
It's like doing a miracle
Which no one in this world can believe
One can only do it absolutely alone
It's like seeing again one's father whom one hasn't seen in thirty-nine years. It's like seeing him come back to the house where we have missed him every day for thirty-nine years, the house has dried up, no one ever watered this heart, one never got over waiting for him with the poisoned teeth of hopeless hope, planted so deeply in the nape of the neck, one remained bitten with death. And now the endless has an end and it's Thursday.

I go back up through Algiers to the Fish Market, a slight exaltation carries me along, for I received an interior gift, while I was in that place where the cypress keeps watch. It's a sentence whose modest appearance hides a paradoxical and thus inexhaustible treasure. "*One can be inconsolable*" it says. I am inconsolable. It is a limitless consolation. In the soul there is an infinity, it is sadness. Sadness is immortally young. I came to Algiers to find once more the immortal sadness. And I found it. It is with me.

It journeys in my journey

What journeys one makes

After the book, I was without either literal or figurative, I was sick with love.

– You know what is happening for me with Algeria? I say to my brother. It has left again. It has fled. I'm delighted I say, I was afraid that it was going to stay. As time is snatched from my mouth, that Algeria be snatched from my mouth. I was afraid. But it has taken flight again. Algeria, the other one, the invented, dreamt one, has all the same managed to carry the day. It carries me off, I say.

Algeria as work of art? No. As Fruit of Times. This Country more beautiful than works of art, richpoor, proudanxious, struckradiant, is not my country. It is my humus. My hyperfunerary stele. I am a pebble of red granite. The tomb keeps me in dreams and sums me up.

I was in Paris but I was not with Paris. I was with Algeria, I was not in Paris, I did not belong to Paris, the essential thing is to have something once again to lose, all the dreams that came to escape me are dreams of Algeria. All the nights in Algeria, like a hallucination, once again the steep slopes the colors, the trees, the white houses, the powers, the seas, *in the place* of dreams, the Algerias, the algereveries, the flows of red granite, the gullies of high houses piled up in the sun, I wake up in the other house, I was in the other book, I am there and I am not there, I flee and don't flee, I leave and she stays there, she leaves and I stay there. So as to begin again – go perhaps to the Jardin d'Essai

Translator's Note

The narrator's memories of childhood and youth in Oran and Algiers are evoked very often in *So Close* by the names of the secondary schools she attended. Given that the school system was, like so much else in Algeria until its independence in 1962, a colonial import from France, these schools are called *lycées* and, what is more, many were named for military figures who played a role in France's conquest of Algeria: General Lamoricière (Christophe Léon Louis Juchault de) fought in the Algerian campaign from 1830 on, where he would have served under Marshall Bugéaud (Thomas Robert, Duc d'Isly), who became Governor-General of Algeria in 1840, where he had under his command General d'Aurelle de Paladines (Louis), whose name would be preserved not by a *lycée* but as the street name in El Biar where the narrator's good friend Jacques Derrida grew up. As for the Lycée Fromentin, it was named for the painter Eugène Fromentin, a contemporary of Delacroix, who was known especially for his paintings of native scenes in Algeria.

But the narrator's French schooling in still-colonial Algeria was also marked by another name and an altogether different figure, that of Zohra Drif, who would have been one of the rare Algerians accorded the privilege of attending the *lycée*. She and the narrator were in the same class for four years in the 1950s. When she was a twenty-year-old law student, Drif joined the FLN (National Liberation Front), and in 1956 was recruited to plant one of the first bombs that targeted the French quarter of Algiers, most memorably at a popular hang-out called the Milk Bar Café. Three persons were killed in that bombing and many injured. Along with the leaders of the insurrection, including Larbi Ben M'hidi, Drif then went into hiding in the Casbah, the oldest Arab neighborhood in Algiers. After the brutal French campaign against the Casbah (depicted in Gillo Pontecorvo's celebrated 1966 film *The Battle of Algiers*), she was captured in 1957 and sentenced to twenty years hard labor. French President de Gaulle pardoned her in 1962 when Algeria won its independence. After the liberation, Drif was elected to the Algerian Senate, where she has remained an influential leader. An English translation of Hélène Cixous's "Letter to Zohra Drif" was first published in 1998.

A final note on the title: *So Close* cannot close the gap in meaning that a French speaker easily detects in *Si près*, where the name of the cypress tree, *cyprès*, can also be heard. Together, these homonyms provide a principal key to the fiction.

– *Peggy Kamuf*

but admittedly,
it time of yogurt covered
pretzels. It am doomed to
monotony even in my life of
Hollywood banditry.

midcity

Hollywood

USC

central table now empties